ESSENTIAL ELEMENTS for Band

COMPREHENSIVE BAND METHOD

TIM LAUTZENHEISER • JOHN HIGGINS • CHARLES MENGHINI
PAUL LAVENDER • TOM C. RHODES • DON BIERSCHENK

Band is...

M aking music with a family of lifelong friends.

U nderstanding how commitment and dedication lead to success.

S haring the joy and rewards of working together.

I ndividuals who develop self-confidence.

C reativity—expressing yourself in a universal language.

Band is...**MUSIC!**

Strike up the band,
Tim Lautzenheiser

HISTORY OF THE BARITONE

Origins of the baritone can be traced to ancient Rome, where bronze and brass instruments called "tubas" often played at military and ceremonial functions. The baritone horn, also known as a tenor tuba, first appeared in Germany in the 1830s. It is the final version of Adolphe Sax's "saxhorn baryton."

The euphonium, closely related to the baritone, was also invented in the 1830s. The tubing of the euphonium is wider (more conically shaped) than the cylindrical tubing of the baritone. Both instruments have 3 or 4 valves and play the same pitches.

Baritones and euphoniums can be played using either bass clef (B.C.) or treble clef (T.C.) fingerings. They are important tenor or bass voiced instruments of the concert band. Baritones play solos and harmonies, and they blend well with other instruments.

John Philip Sousa, Percy Grainger and Alfred Reed are important composers who have included baritones in their concert band writing. Some famous baritone performers are Leonard Falcone, Brian Bowman and Rich Matteson.

To create an account, visit:
www.essentialelementsinteractive.com
Student Activation Code
E1BB-5405-0679-8214

ISBN 979-835012068-4

THE BASICS

Posture

Sit on the edge of your chair, and always keep your:

- Spine straight and tall
- Shoulders back and relaxed
- Feet flat on the floor

Breathing & Airstream

Breathing is a natural thing we all do constantly. To discover the correct airstream to play your instrument:

- Place the palm of your hand near your mouth.
- Inhale deeply through the corners of your mouth, keeping your shoulders steady. Your waist should expand like a balloon.
- Slowly whisper "tah" as you gradually exhale air into your palm.

The air you feel is the airstream. It produces sound through the instrument. Your tongue is like a faucet or valve that releases the airstream.

Producing The Essential Tone

"Buzzing" through the mouthpiece produces your tone. The buzz is a fast vibration in the center of your lips. Your embouchure (*ahm'-bah-shure*) is your mouth's position on the mouthpiece of the instrument. A good embouchure takes time and effort, so carefully follow these steps for success:

BUZZING

- Moisten your lips.
- Bring your lips together as if saying the letter "m."
- Relax your jaw to separate your upper and lower teeth.
- Form a slightly puckered smile to firm the corners of your mouth.
- Direct a full airstream through the center of your lips, creating a buzz.
- Buzz frequently without your mouthpiece.

MOUTHPIECE PLACEMENT

- Form your "buzzing" embouchure.
- Place the mouthpiece approximately 2/3 on the upper lip and 1/3 on the lower lip. Your teacher may suggest a slightly different mouthpiece placement.
- Take a full breath through the corners of your mouth.
- Start your buzz with the syllable "tah." Buzz through the center of your lips keeping a steady, even buzz. Your lips provide a cushion for the mouthpiece.

Taking Care Of Your Instrument

Before putting your instrument back in its case after playing, do the following:

- Use the water key to empty water from the instrument. Blow air through it.
- Remove the mouthpiece. Once a week, wash the mouthpiece with warm tap water. Dry thoroughly.
- Wipe off the instrument with a clean soft cloth. Return the instrument to its case.

Baritone valves occasionally need oiling. To oil your baritone valves:

- Unscrew the valve at the top of the casing.
- Lift the valve half-way out of the casing.
- Apply a few drops of special brass valve oil to the exposed valve.
- Carefully return the valve to its casing. When properly inserted, the top of the valve should easily screw back into place.

Be sure to grease the slides regularly. Your director will recommend special slide grease and valve oil, and will help you apply them when necessary.

MOUTHPIECE WORKOUT

Using only the mouthpiece, form your embouchure carefully. Take a deep breath without raising your shoulders. Begin buzzing your lips by whispering "tah" and gradually exhale your full airstream. Strive for an even tone.

REST

Getting It Together

Step 1 Rest the baritone across your lap so the bell faces upward and the mouthpiece receiver points toward you.

Step 2 Carefully twist the mouthpiece to the right into the mouthpiece receiver.

Step 3 Place your right thumb in the thumb ring. Rest your fingertips on top of the valves, keeping your wrist straight. Your fingers should curve naturally.

Step 4 Place your left hand on the third valve slide or on the tubing next to this slide. Lift the instrument up toward you.

Step 5 Be sure you can comfortably reach the mouthpiece. Hold the baritone as shown:

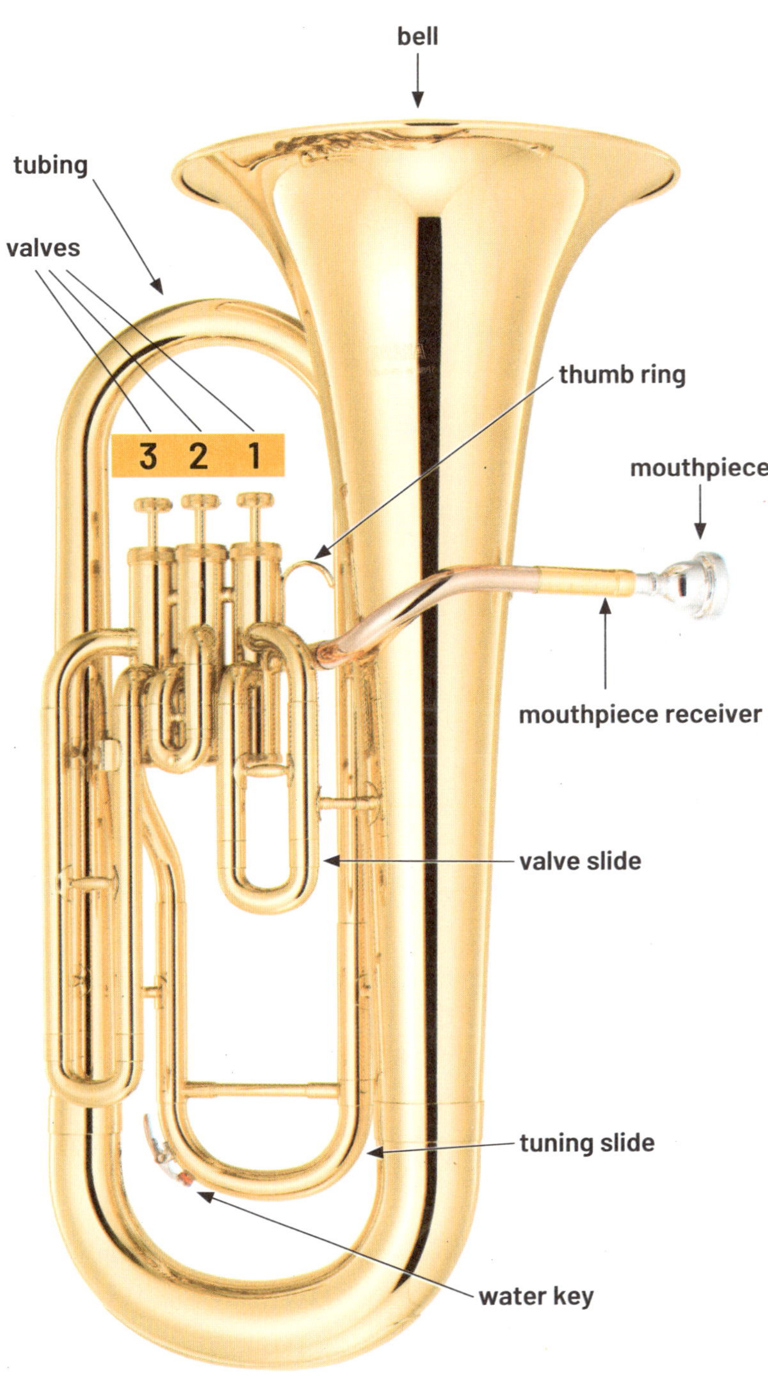

The student shown is a member of the Milwaukee Youth Symphony Orchestra.

READING MUSIC

Identify and draw each of these symbols:

Music Staff

The **music staff** has 5 lines and 4 spaces where notes and rests are written.

Ledger Lines

Ledger lines extend the music staff. Notes on ledger lines can be above or below the staff.

Measures & Bar Lines

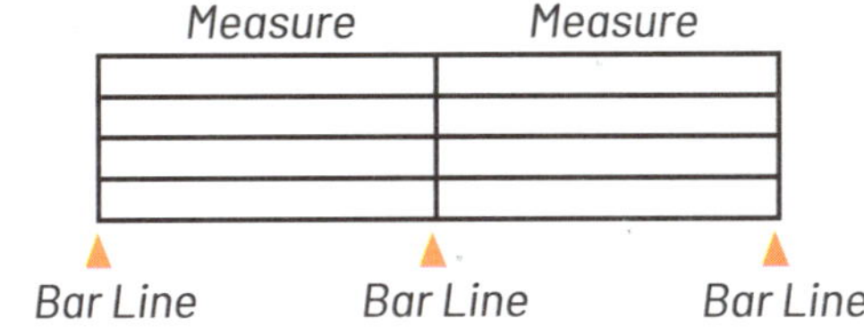

Bar lines divide the music staff into **measures**.

See inside front cover for information on accessing instructional videos.

Long Tone 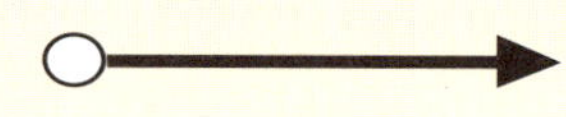 To begin, we'll use a special "Long Tone" note. Hold the tone until your teacher tells you to rest. Practice long tones each day to develop your sound.

1. THE FIRST NOTE

Hold each long tone until your teacher tells you to rest.

F

○○○
1 2 3

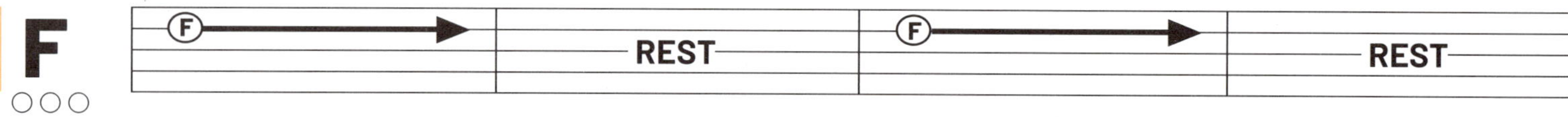

*"F" is played with **open valves**. Just rest your fingers lightly on the valves.*

The Beat

The **beat** is the pulse of music, and like your heartbeat it should remain very steady. Counting aloud and foot-tapping help us maintain a steady beat. Tap your foot **down** on each number and **up** on each "&."

One beat = 1 &
↓ ↑

Notes & Rests

Notes tell us how high or low to play by their placement on a line or space of the music staff, and how long to play by their shape. **Rests** tell us to count silent beats.

Quarter Note = 1 beat

Quarter Rest = 1 silent beat

2. COUNT AND PLAY

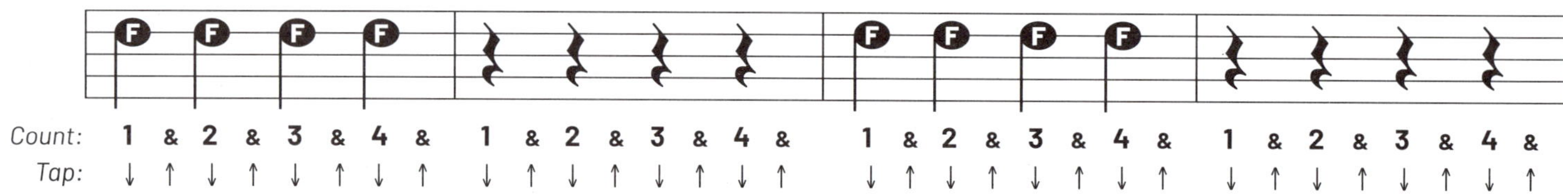

3. A NEW NOTE

Look for the fingering diagram under each new note.

E♭

●○○

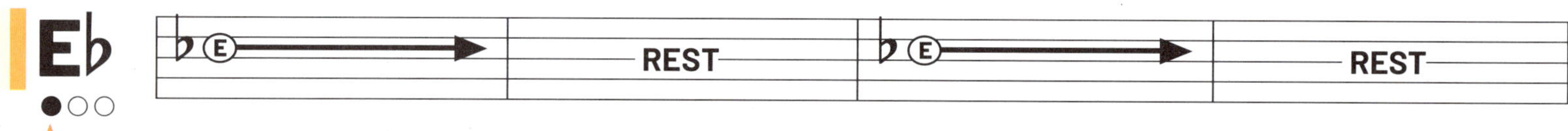

*The black circles tell you which valves to push down. "E♭ (E-flat)" is played with **1st valve**.*

4. TWO'S A TEAM

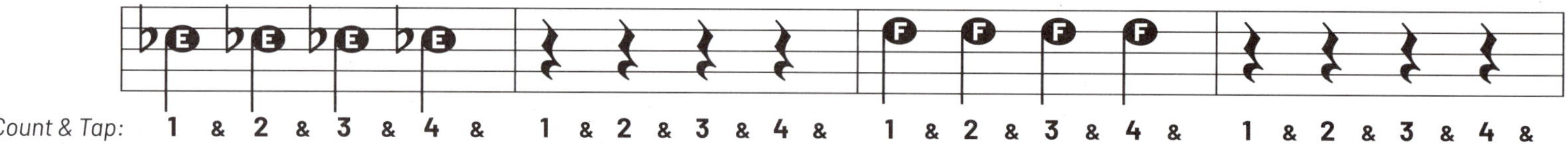

5. HEADING DOWN

Practice long tones on each new note.

D

●●○

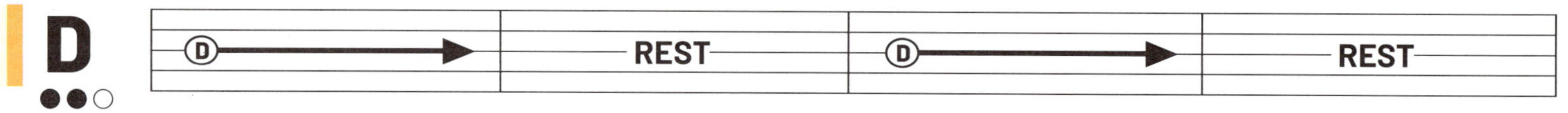

6. MOVING ON UP

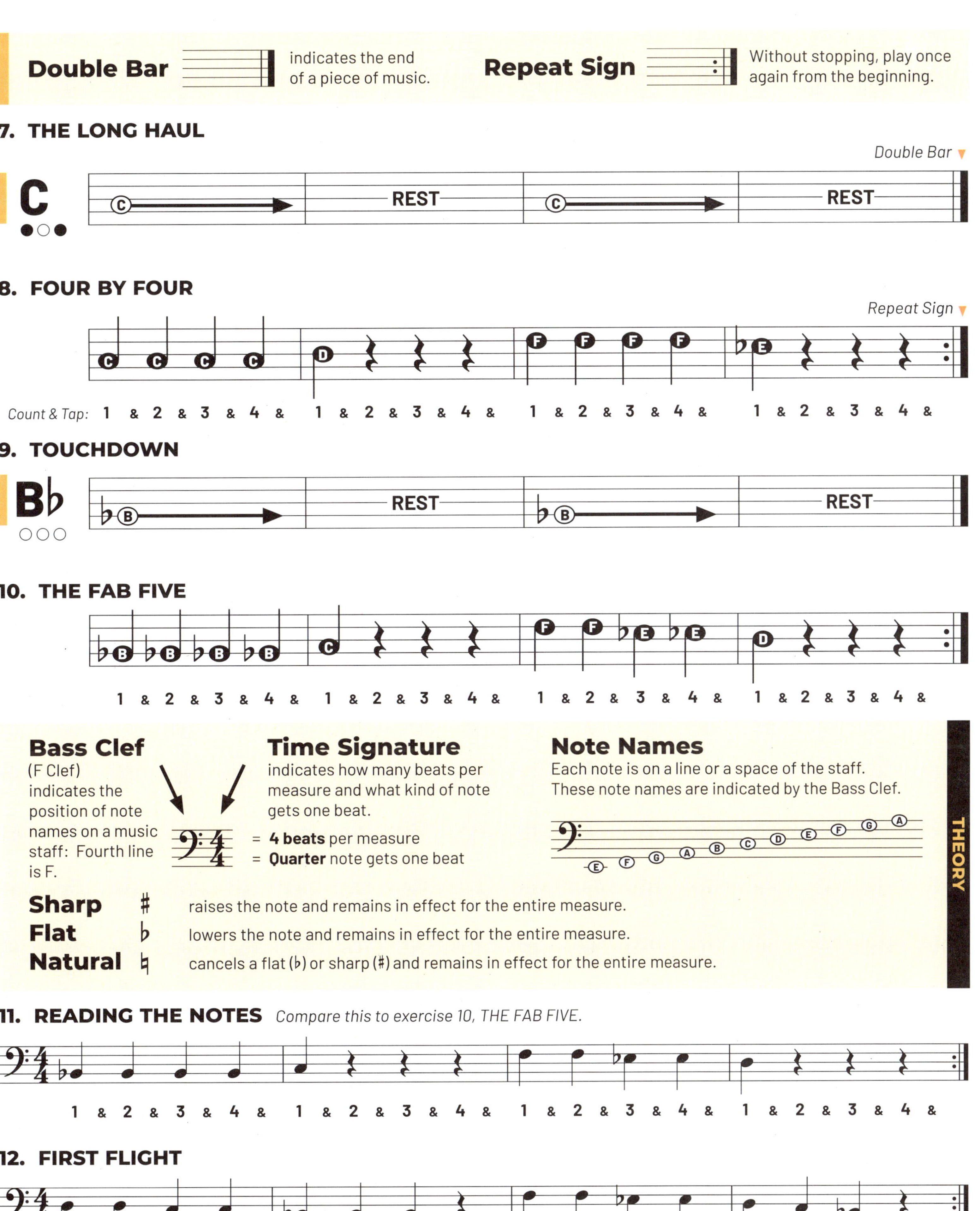

13. ESSENTIAL ELEMENTS QUIZ

Fill in the remaining note names before playing.

B♭ C D ___ ___ ___ ___ ___ ___ ___ ___ ___ ___ ___ ___

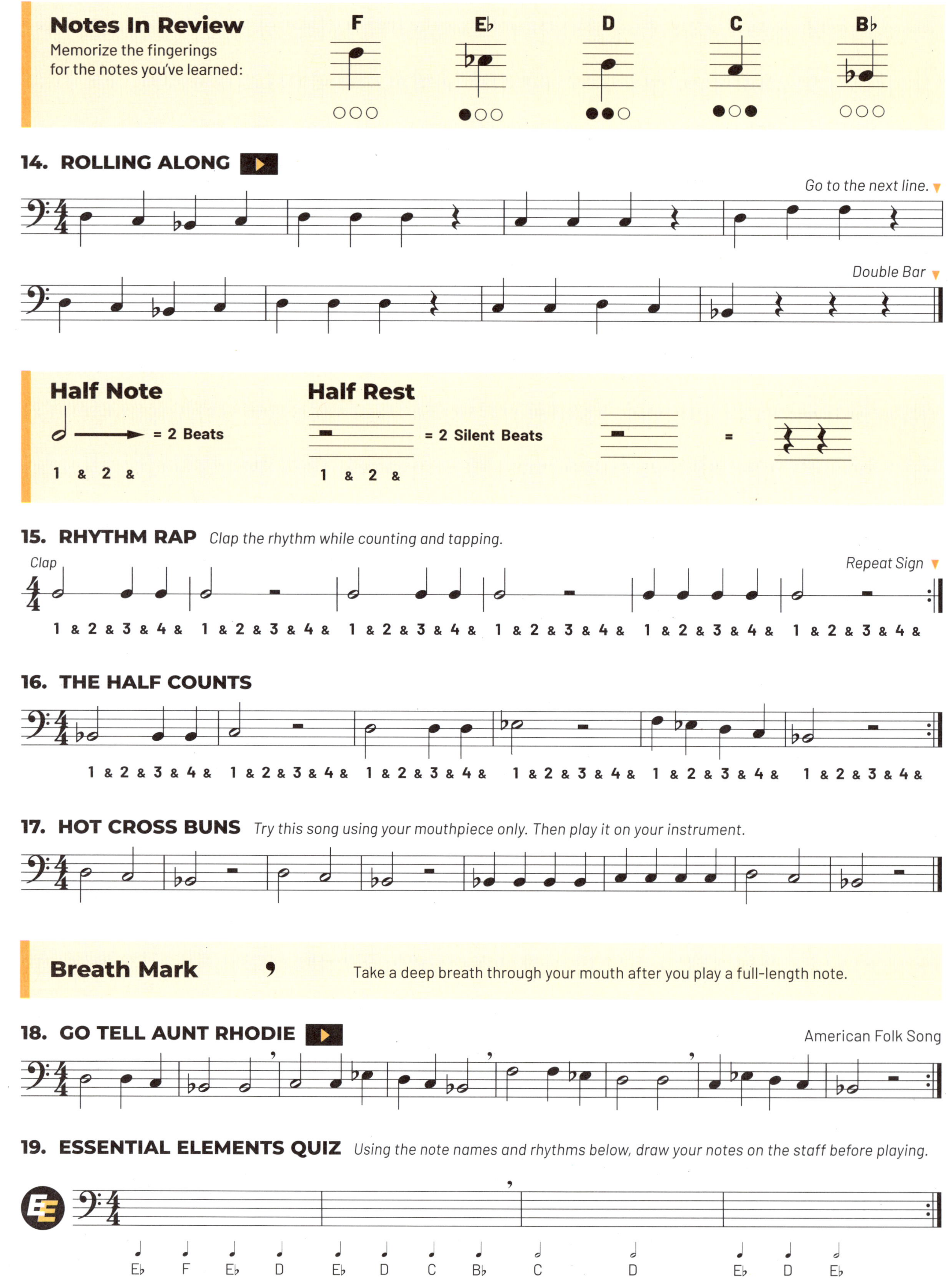
Notes In Review
Memorize the fingerings for the notes you've learned:
F
E♭
D
C
B♭
14. ROLLING ALONG
Go to the next line.
Double Bar
Half Note
= 2 Beats
1 & 2 &
Half Rest
= 2 Silent Beats
1 & 2 &
=
15. RHYTHM RAP Clap the rhythm while counting and tapping.
Clap
Repeat Sign
1 & 2 & 3 & 4 & 1 & 2 & 3 & 4 & 1 & 2 & 3 & 4 & 1 & 2 & 3 & 4 & 1 & 2 & 3 & 4 & 1 & 2 & 3 & 4 &
16. THE HALF COUNTS
1 & 2 & 3 & 4 & 1 & 2 & 3 & 4 & 1 & 2 & 3 & 4 & 1 & 2 & 3 & 4 & 1 & 2 & 3 & 4 & 1 & 2 & 3 & 4 &
17. HOT CROSS BUNS Try this song using your mouthpiece only. Then play it on your instrument.
Breath Mark
Take a deep breath through your mouth after you play a full-length note.
18. GO TELL AUNT RHODIE
American Folk Song
19. ESSENTIAL ELEMENTS QUIZ Using the note names and rhythms below, draw your notes on the staff before playing.
E♭ F E♭ D E♭ D C B♭ C D E♭ D E♭

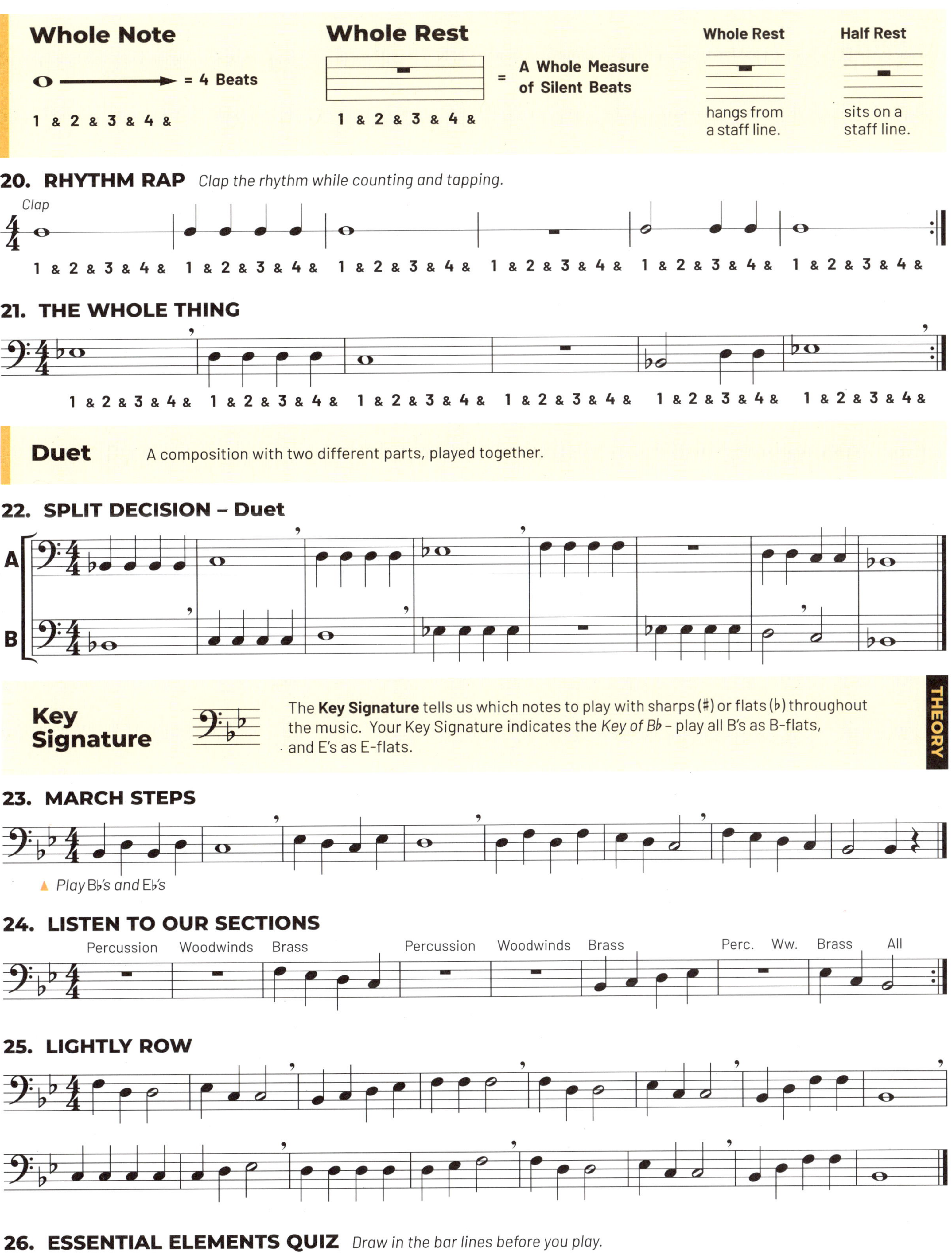
Whole Note
= 4 Beats
1 & 2 & 3 & 4 &
Whole Rest
= A Whole Measure of Silent Beats
1 & 2 & 3 & 4 &
Whole Rest
hangs from a staff line.
Half Rest
sits on a staff line.
20. RHYTHM RAP Clap the rhythm while counting and tapping.
Clap
1 & 2 & 3 & 4 & 1 & 2 & 3 & 4 & 1 & 2 & 3 & 4 & 1 & 2 & 3 & 4 & 1 & 2 & 3 & 4 & 1 & 2 & 3 & 4 &
21. THE WHOLE THING
1 & 2 & 3 & 4 & 1 & 2 & 3 & 4 & 1 & 2 & 3 & 4 & 1 & 2 & 3 & 4 & 1 & 2 & 3 & 4 & 1 & 2 & 3 & 4 &
Duet
A composition with two different parts, played together.
22. SPLIT DECISION – Duet
A
B
Key Signature
The Key Signature tells us which notes to play with sharps (♯) or flats (♭) throughout the music. Your Key Signature indicates the Key of B♭ – play all B's as B-flats, and E's as E-flats.
THEORY
23. MARCH STEPS
Play B♭'s and E♭'s
24. LISTEN TO OUR SECTIONS
Percussion
Woodwinds
Brass
Percussion
Woodwinds
Brass
Perc.
Ww.
Brass
All
25. LIGHTLY ROW
26. ESSENTIAL ELEMENTS QUIZ Draw in the bar lines before you play.
EE

Fermata 𝄐 Hold the note (or rest) longer than normal.

27. REACHING HIGHER – New Note

Practice long tones on each new note.

Fermata ▼

28. AU CLAIRE DE LA LUNE

French Folk Song

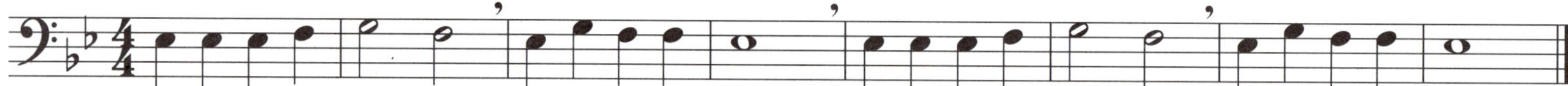

29. REMIX

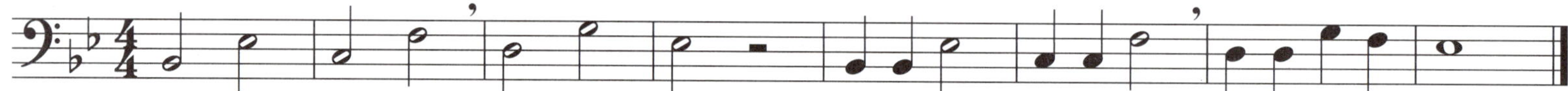

THEORY

Harmony Two or more notes played together. Each combination forms a *chord*.

30. LONDON BRIDGE – Duet

English Folk Song

HISTORY

Austrian composer **Wolfgang Amadeus Mozart** (1756–1791) was a child prodigy who started playing professionally at age six, and lived during the time of the American Revolution. Mozart's music is melodic and imaginative. He wrote more than 600 compositions during his short life, including a piano piece based on the famous song, "Twinkle, Twinkle, Little Star."

31. A MOZART MELODY

Adaptation

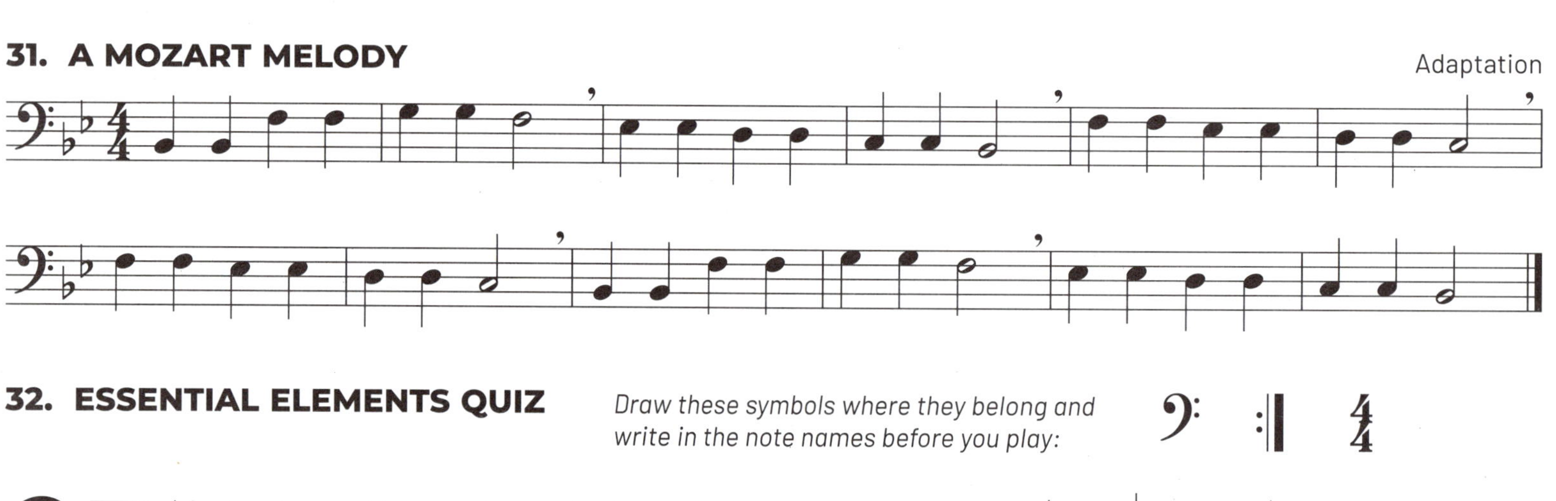

32. ESSENTIAL ELEMENTS QUIZ

Draw these symbols where they belong and write in the note names before you play:

▲ ▲ __ __ __ __ __ __ __ __ __ __ __ __ ▲

33. DEEP POCKETS – New Note

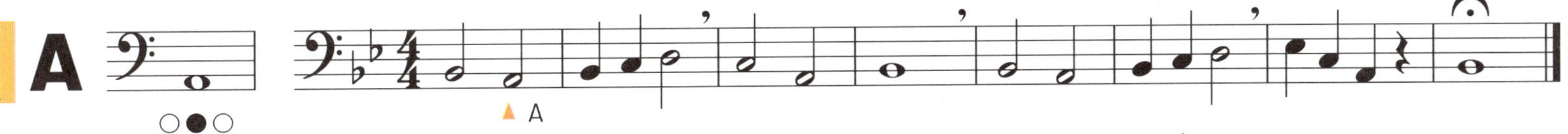

34. DOODLE ALL DAY

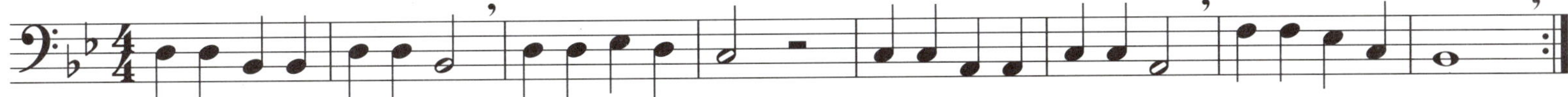

35. JUMP ROPE

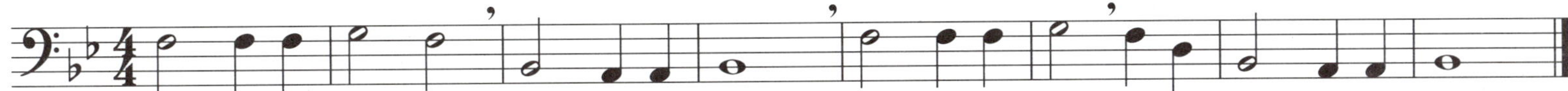

Pick-Up Notes One or more notes that come before the first *full* measure. The beats of Pick-Up Notes are subtracted from the last measure.

36. A-TISKET, A-TASKET

Dynamics ***f*** – *forte* (play loudly) ***mf*** – *mezzo forte* (play moderately loud) ***p*** – *piano* (play softly)
Remember to use full breath support to control your tone at all dynamic levels.

37. LOUD AND SOFT

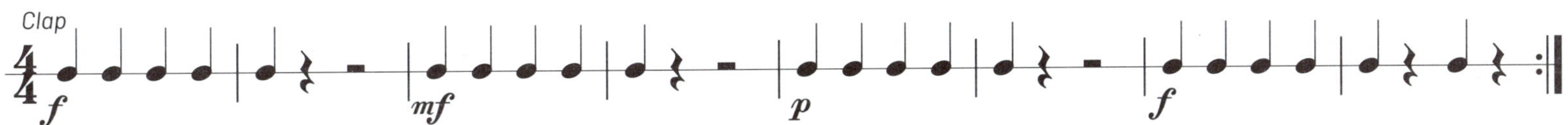

38. JINGLE BELLS *Also practice new music on your mouthpiece only.*

J. S. Pierpont

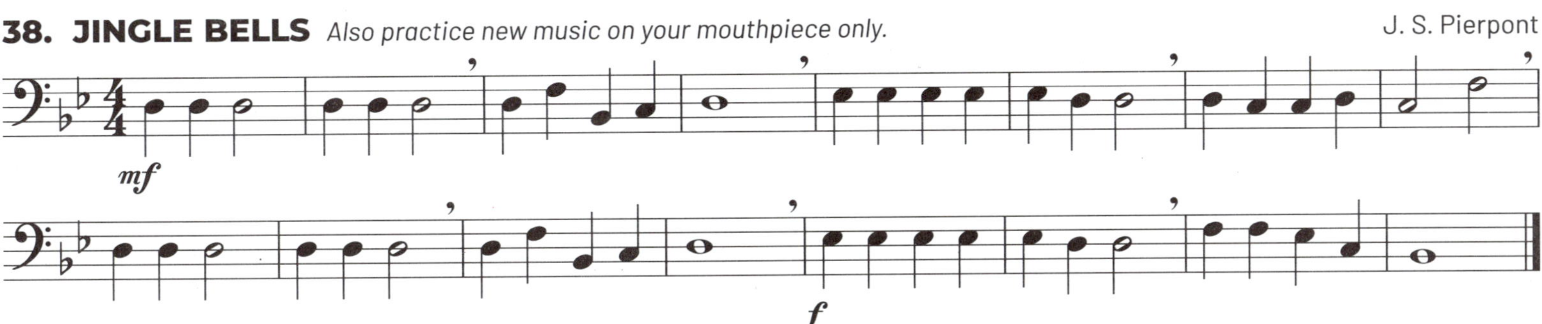

39. MY DREYDL *Use full breath support at all dynamic levels.*

Traditional Hanukkah Song

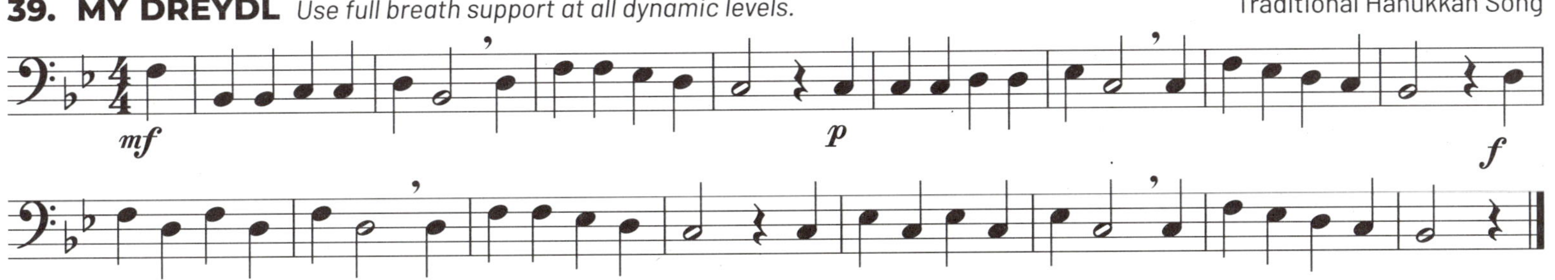

Eighth Notes

40. RHYTHM RAP *Clap the rhythm while counting and tapping.*

41. EIGHTH NOTE JAM

42. SKIP TO MY LOU

American Folk Song

43. LONG, LONG AGO *Good posture improves your sound. Always sit straight and tall.*

44. CANDY MOUNTAIN ROCK

HISTORY

Italian composer **Gioachino Rossini** (1792–1868) began composing as a teenager and was very proficient on the piano, viola and horn. He wrote "William Tell" at age 37 as the last of his forty operas, and its familiar theme is still heard today on radio and television.

45. ESSENTIAL ELEMENTS QUIZ – WILLIAM TELL

Gioachino Rossini

2/4 Time Signature

2/4 = **2 beats** per measure
= **Quarter** note gets one beat

Conducting

Practice conducting this two-beat pattern.

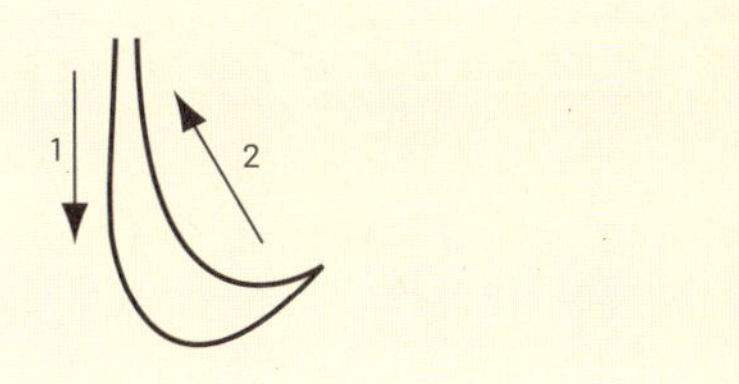

THEORY

46. RHYTHM RAP

47. TWO BY TWO

Tempo Markings

Tempo is the speed of music. Tempo markings are usually written above the staff, in Italian.
Allegro – Fast tempo **Moderato** – Medium tempo **Andante** – Slower walking tempo

48. HIGH SCHOOL CADETS – March

John Philip Sousa

49. HEY, HO! NOBODY'S HOME

Dynamics

Crescendo (gradually louder)
Decrescendo or *Diminuendo* (gradually softer)

50. CLAP THE DYNAMICS

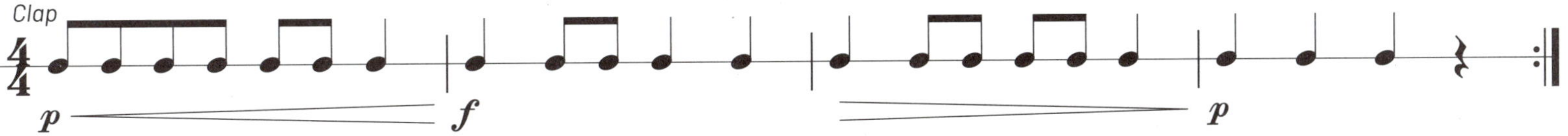

51. PLAY THE DYNAMICS

Looking for some more fun music to play?
See the inside front cover for instructions on accessing recent popular Bonus Songs.

PERFORMANCE SPOTLIGHT

52. PERFORMANCE WARM-UPS

53. AURA LEE – Duet or Band Arrangement

(Part A = Melody, Part B = Harmony)

George R. Poulton

54. FRÈRE JACQUES – Round *(When group A reaches ②, group B begins at ①)*

French Folk Song

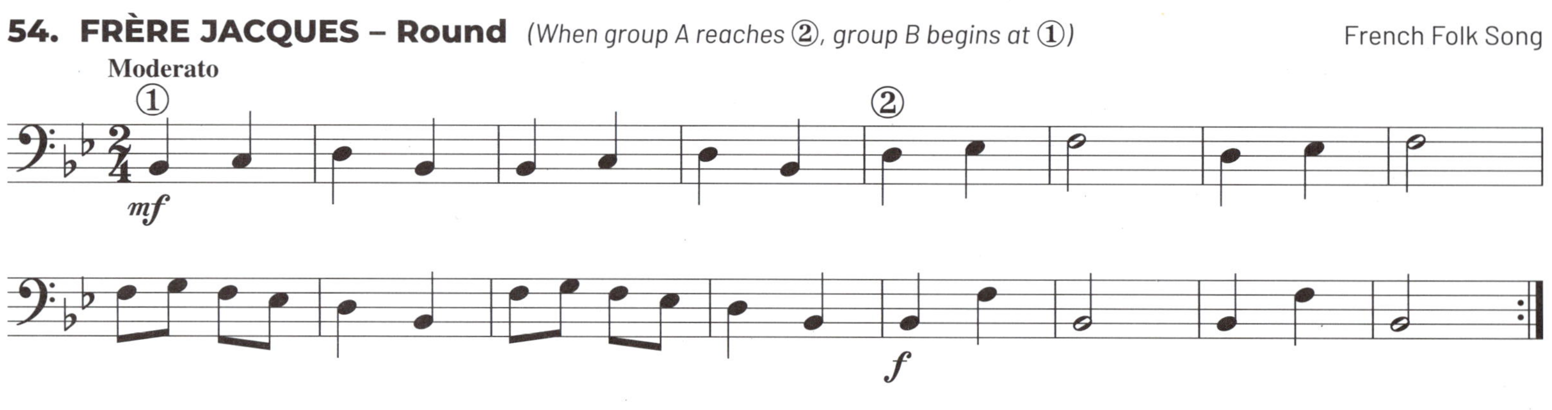

PERFORMANCE SPOTLIGHT

Tie

A curved line connecting notes of the same pitch.
Play one note for the combined counts of the tied notes.

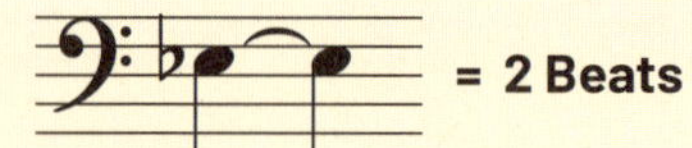

59. FIT TO BE TIED

60. ALOUETTE

French-Canadian Folk Song

Dotted Half Note

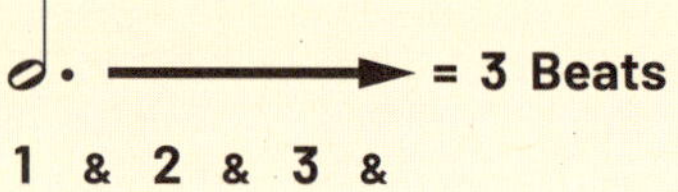

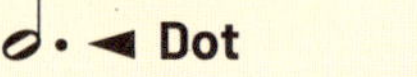

A dot adds half the value of the note.

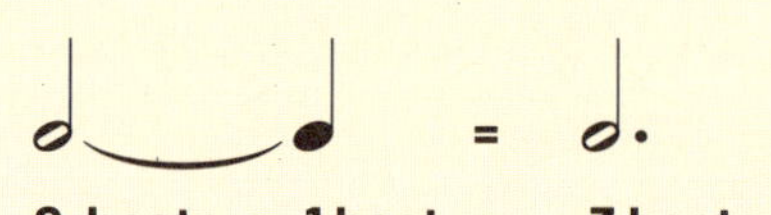

61. ALOUETTE – THE SEQUEL

French-Canadian Folk Song

62. IT'S RAINING

63. NEW DIRECTIONS

64. THE NOBLES

Always use a full airstream. Keep fingers on top of the valves, arched naturally.

65. ESSENTIAL ELEMENTS QUIZ

3/4 Time Signature

= **3 beats** per measure
= **Quarter** note gets one beat

Conducting

Practice conducting this three-beat pattern.

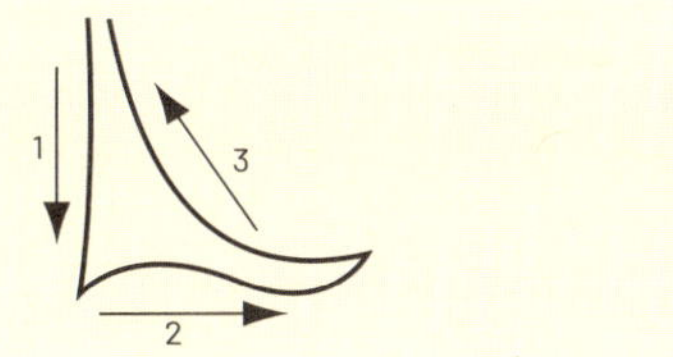

THEORY

66. RHYTHM RAP

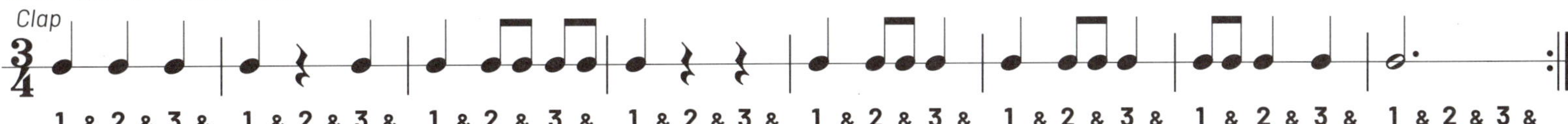

67. THREE BEAT JAM

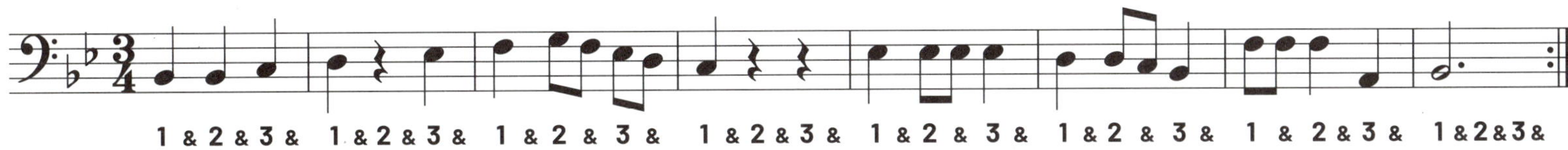

68. BARCAROLLE

Jacques Offenbach

Norwegian composer **Edvard Grieg** (1843–1907) wrote *Peer Gynt Suite* for a play by Henrik Ibsen in 1875, the year before the telephone was invented by Alexander Graham Bell. "Morning" is a melody from *Peer Gynt Suite*. Music used in plays, or in films and television, is called **incidental music**.

HISTORY

69. MORNING (from Peer Gynt)

Edvard Grieg

Accent

Emphasize the note.

70. ACCENT YOUR TALENT

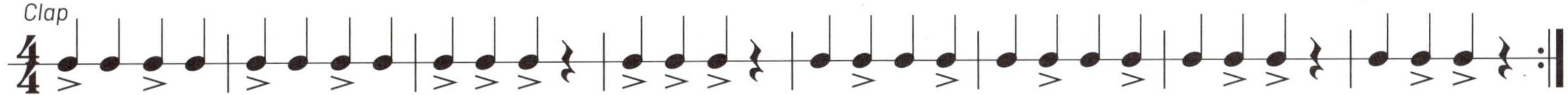

Latin American music has its roots in the African, Native American, Spanish and Portuguese cultures. This diverse music features lively accompaniments by drums and other percussion instruments such as maracas and claves. Music from Latin America continues to influence jazz, classical and popular styles of music. "Chiapanecas" is a popular children's dance and game song.

71. MEXICAN CLAPPING SONG ("Chiapanecas")

Latin American Folk Song

72. ESSENTIAL CREATIVITY

Compose your own music for measures 3 and 4 using this rhythm:

THEORY

Accidental

Any sharp, flat or natural sign which appears in the music without being in the key signature is called an **accidental**.

Flat ♭

A **flat** sign lowers the pitch of a note by a half-step. The note A-flat sounds a half-step below A, and all A's become A-flats for the rest of the measure where they occur.

73. HOT MUFFINS – New Note

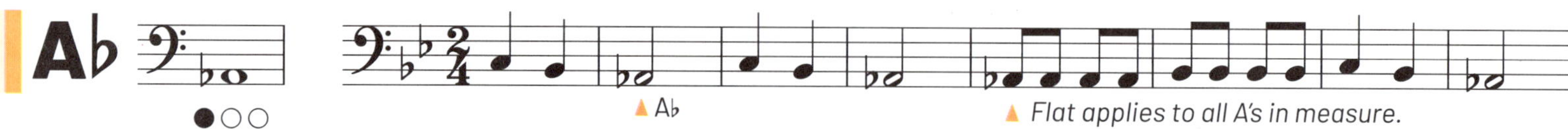

74. COSSACK DANCE

75. BASIC BLUES – New Note

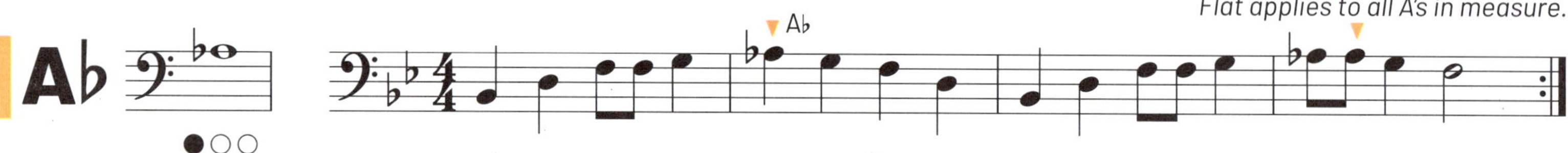

THEORY

New Key Signature

This Key Signature indicates the *Key of E♭* – play all B's as B-flats, all E's as E-flats, and all A's as A-flats.

1st & 2nd Endings

1. 2.

Play through the 1st Ending.
Then play the repeated section of music, **skipping** the 1st Ending and playing the 2nd Ending.

76. HIGH FLYING

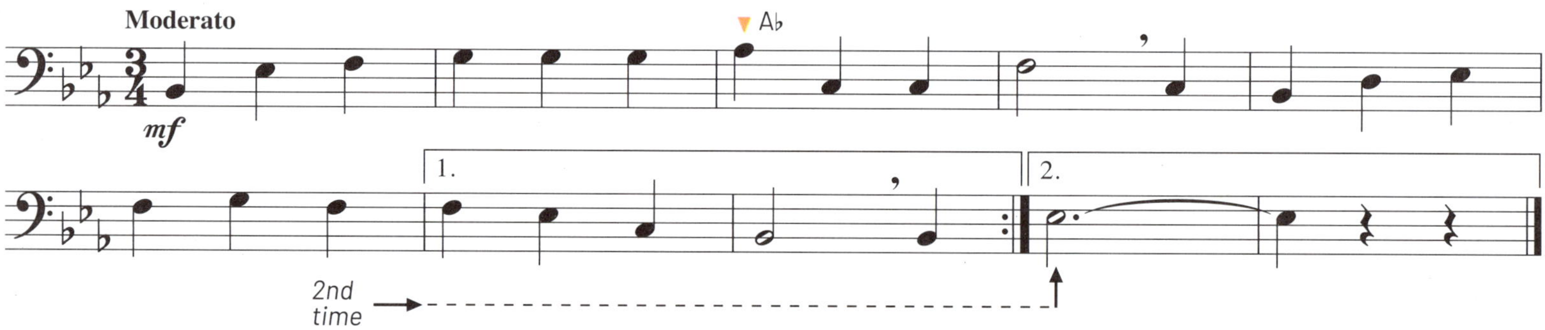

HISTORY

Japanese folk music actually has its origins in ancient China. "Sakura, Sakura" was performed on instruments such as the **koto**, a 13-string instrument that is more than 4000 years old, and the **shakuhachi** or bamboo flute. The unique sound of this ancient Japanese melody results from the pentatonic (or five-note) sequence used in this tonal system.

77. SAKURA, SAKURA – Band Arrangement

Japanese Folk Song
Arr. by John Higgins

78. UP ON A HOUSETOP

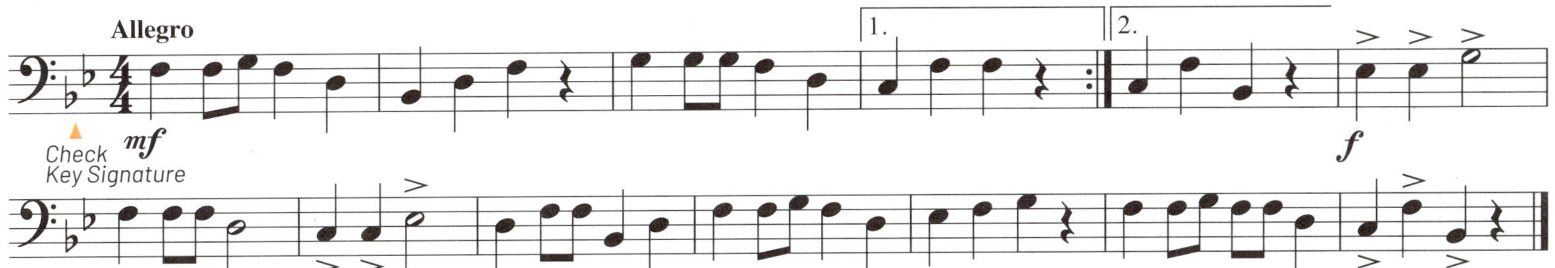

79. JOLLY OLD ST. NICK – Duet

See page 9 for additional holiday music, MY DREYDL and JINGLE BELLS.

80. THE BIG AIRSTREAM – New Note

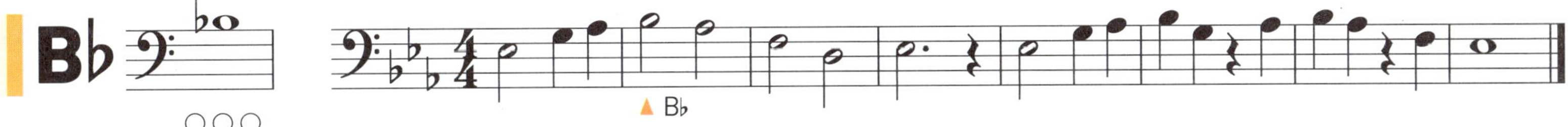

81. WALTZ THEME (THE MERRY WIDOW WALTZ)

Franz Lehar

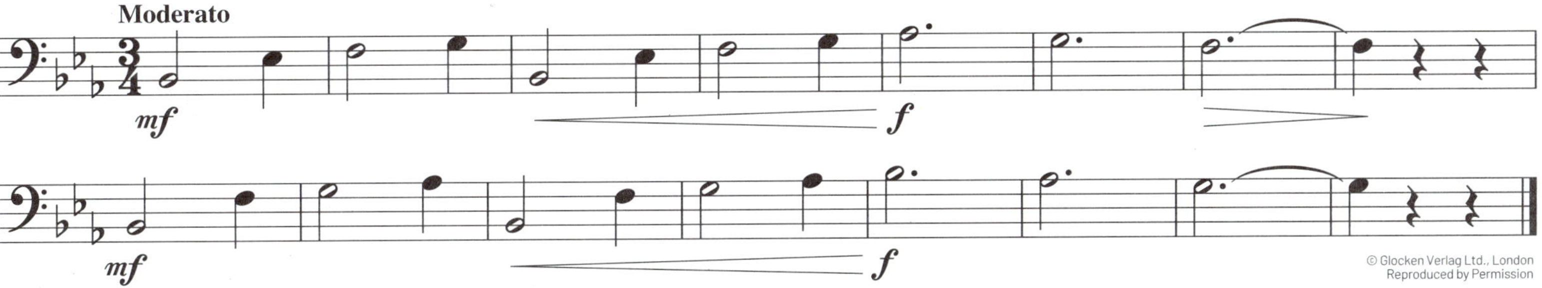

82. AIR TIME

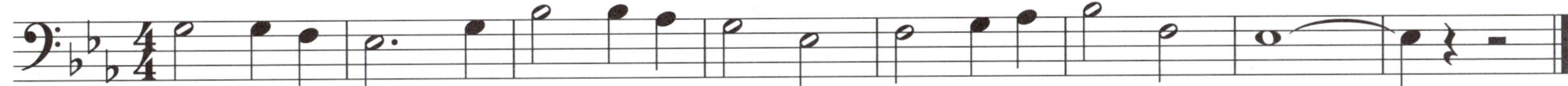

83. DOWN BY THE STATION

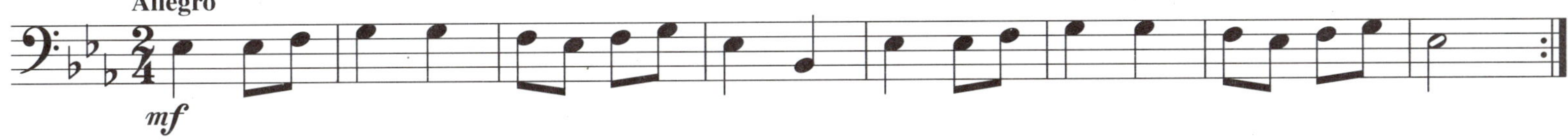

84. ESSENTIAL ELEMENTS QUIZ

85. ESSENTIAL CREATIVITY *Using these notes, improvise your own rhythms:*

DAILY WARM-UPS

WORK-OUTS FOR TONE & TECHNIQUE

86. TONE BUILDER *Use a steady stream of air.*

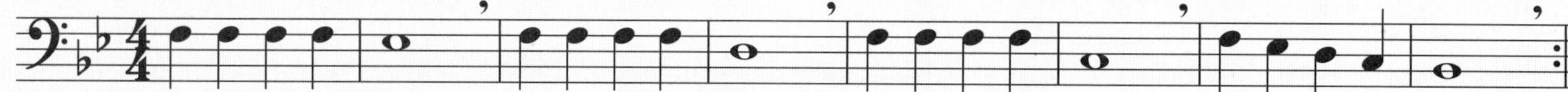

87. RHYTHM BUILDER

88. TECHNIQUE TRAX

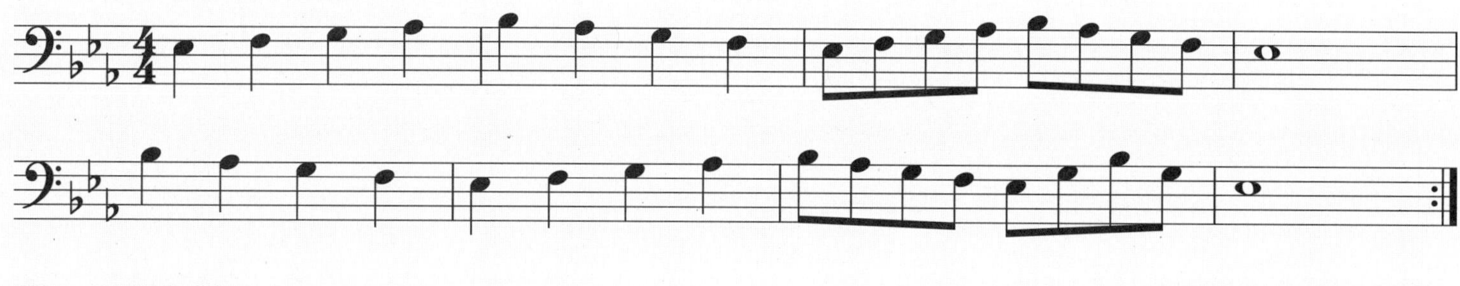

89. CHORALE *(Adapted from Cantata 147)*

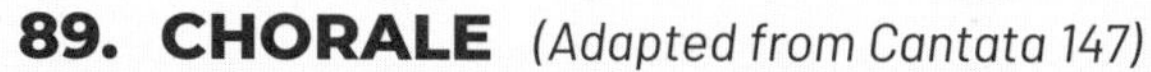

Johann Sebastian Bach

THEORY

Theme and Variations

A musical form featuring a **theme**, or primary melody, followed by **variations**, or altered versions of the theme.

90. VARIATIONS ON A FAMILIAR THEME

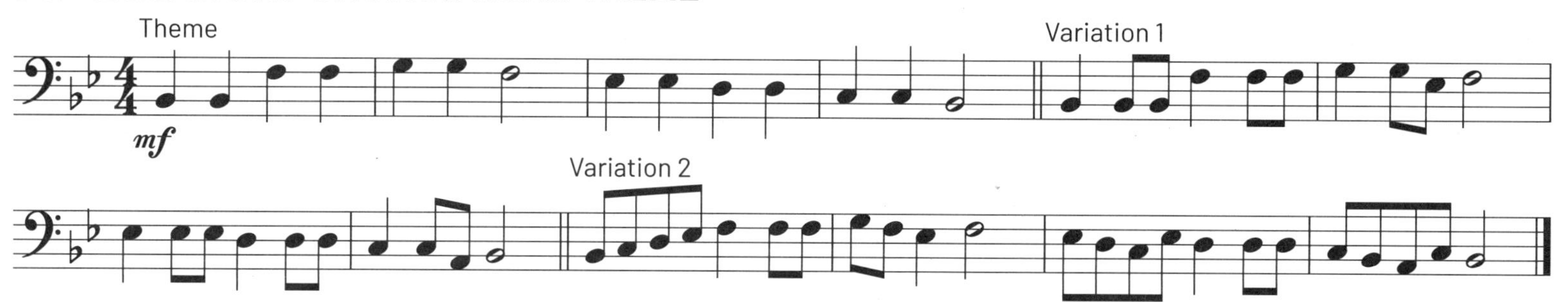

D.C. al Fine

At the **D.C. al Fine** play again from the beginning, stopping at **Fine** *(fee'- nay)*. **D.C.** is the abbreviation for **Da Capo**, or "to the beginning," and **Fine** means "the end."

91. BANANA BOAT SONG

Caribbean Folk Song

Natural ♮

THEORY

A **natural** sign cancels a flat (♭) or sharp (♯) and remains in effect for the entire measure.

92. RAZOR'S EDGE – New Note

93. THE MUSIC BOX

HISTORY

African-American spirituals originated in the 1700's, midway through the period of slavery in the United States. One of the largest categories of true American folk music, these primarily religious songs were sung and passed on for generations without being written down. The first collection of spirituals was published in 1867, four years after The Emancipation Proclamation was signed into law.

94. EZEKIEL SAW THE WHEEL

African-American Spiritual

Slur A curved line which connects notes of different pitch. Tongue only the first note in a **slur**.

95. SMOOTH OPERATOR

▲ *Slur 2 notes – tongue only the first.*

96. GLIDING ALONG

▲ *Slur 4 notes – tongue only the first.*

HISTORY

Ragtime is an American music style that was popular from the 1890's until the time of World War I. This early form of jazz brought fame to pianists like "Jelly Roll" Morton and Scott Joplin, who wrote "The Entertainer" and "Maple Leaf Rag." Surprisingly, the style was incorporated into some orchestral music by Igor Stravinsky and Claude Debussy. The trombones learn how to play a *glissando*, a technique used in ragtime and other styles of music.

97. TROMBONE RAG

98. ESSENTIAL ELEMENTS QUIZ

99. TAKE THE LEAD – New Note

THEORY

Phrase A musical "sentence" which is often 2 or 4 measures long. Try to play a **phrase** in one breath.

100. THE COLD WIND

101. PHRASEOLOGY *Write in the breath mark(s) between the phrases.*

THEORY

New Key Signature

This **Key Signature** indicates the *Key of F* – play all B's as B-flats.

Multiple Measure Rest

The number above the staff tells you how many full measures to rest.
Count each measure of rest in sequence: **1**-2-3-4 **2**-2-3-4

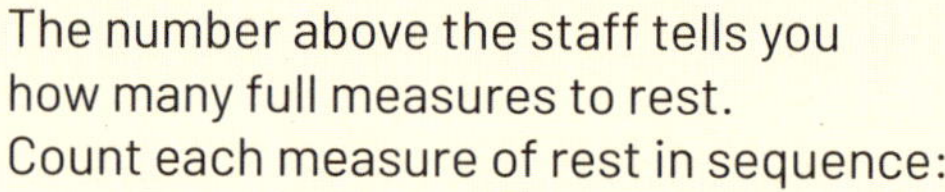

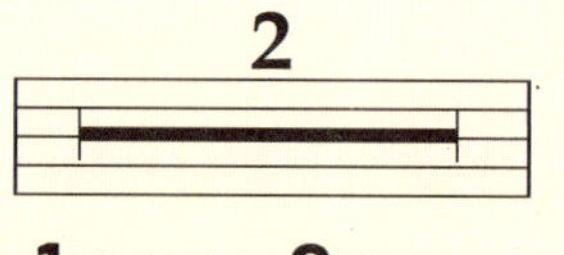

102. SATIN LATIN

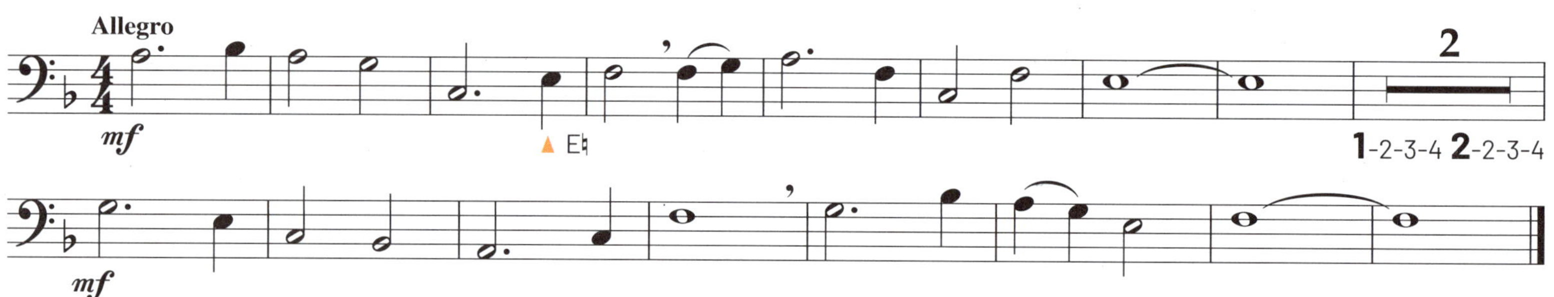

HISTORY

German composer **Johann Sebastian Bach** (1685–1750) was part of a large family of famous musicians and became the most recognized composer of the Baroque era. Beginning as a choir member, Bach soon became an organist, a teacher, and a prolific composer, writing more than 600 masterworks. This *Minuet*, or dance in 3/4 time, was written as a teaching piece for use with an early form of the piano.

103. MINUET – Duet

Johann Sebastian Bach

104. ESSENTIAL CREATIVITY *This melody can be played in 3/4 or 4/4. Pencil in either time signature, draw the bar lines and play. Now erase the bar lines and try the other time signature. Do the phrases sound different?*

105. NATURALLY

Austrian composer **Franz Peter Schubert** (1797–1828) lived a shorter life than any other great composer, but he created an incredible amount of music: more than 600 art-songs (concert music for voice and accompaniment), ten symphonies, chamber music, operas, choral works and piano pieces. His "March Militaire" was originally a piano duet.

HISTORY

106. MARCH MILITAIRE

Franz Schubert

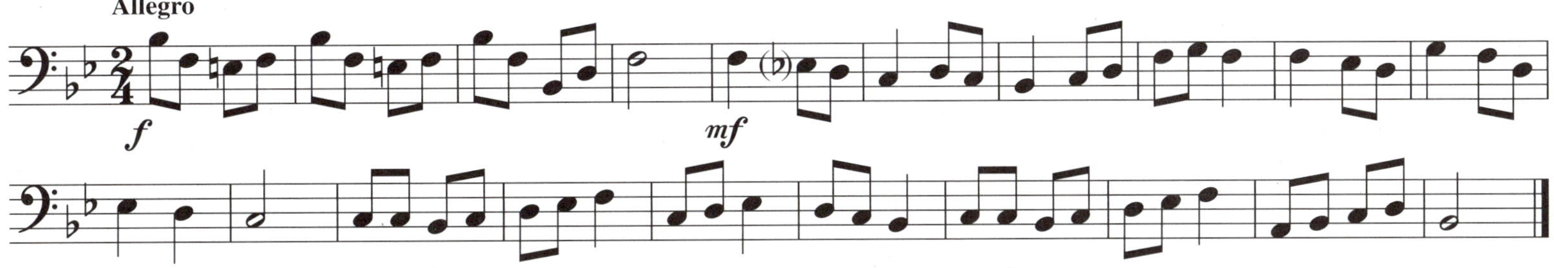

107. THE FLAT ZONE – New Note

D♭

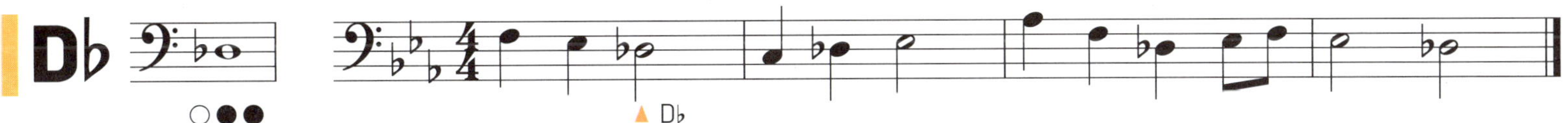

108. ON TOP OF OLD SMOKEY

American Folk Song

Boogie-woogie is a style of the **blues**, and it was first recorded by pianist Clarence "Pine Top" Smith in 1928, one year after Charles Lindbergh's solo flight across the Atlantic. A form of jazz, blues music features altered notes and is usually written in 12-measure verses, like "Bottom Bass Boogie."

HISTORY

109. BOTTOM BASS BOOGIE – Duet

Dotted Quarter & Eighth Notes
= 2 Beats
1 & 2 &
A dot adds half the value of the quarter note.
1 & 2 &
A single eighth note has a flag on the stem.
110. RHYTHM RAP
Clap
1 & 2 & 3 & 4 & 1 & 2 & 3 & 4 & 1 & 2 & 3 & 4 & 1 & 2 & 3 & 4 &
111. THE DOT ALWAYS COUNTS
1 & 2 & 3 & 4 & 1 & 2 & 3 & 4 & 1 & 2 & 3 & 4 & 1 & 2 & 3 & 4 &
112. ALL THROUGH THE NIGHT
Fine
D.C. al Fine
mf
p
113. SEA CHANTY Always use a full airstream.
English Folk Song
Moderato
f
mf
f
114. SCARBOROUGH FAIR
English Folk Song
Andante
mf
f
mf
p
115. RHYTHM RAP
Clap
1 & 2 & 3 & 4 & 1 & 2 & 3 & 4 & 1 & 2 & 3 & 4 & 1 & 2 & 3 & 4 &
116. THE TURNAROUND
1 & 2 & 3 & 4 & 1 & 2 & 3 & 4 & 1 & 2 & 3 & 4 & 1 & 2 & 3 & 4 &
117. ESSENTIAL ELEMENTS QUIZ – AULD LANG SYNE
Scottish Folk Song
Andante
EE
mf
Check Rhythm
f

PERFORMANCE SPOTLIGHT

Solo with Piano Accompaniment

You can perform this solo with or without a piano accompanist. Play it for the band, the school or your family. It is part of **Symphony No. 9 ("From The New World")** by Czech composer **Antonin Dvorák** (1841–1904). He wrote it while visiting America in 1893, and was inspired to include melodies from American folksongs and spirituals. This is the **Largo** (or "very slow tempo") theme.

118. THEME FROM "NEW WORLD SYMPHONY"

Antonin Dvorák

SPECIAL BARITONE EXERCISE – Lip Slurs

Lip Slurs are notes that are slurred without changing valves. Brass players practice these to develop a stronger airstream and embouchure, and to increase range. Add this pattern to your daily Warm-Ups:

Great musicians give encouragement to fellow performers. On this page, clarinetists learn their instruments' upper register in the "Grenadilla Gorilla Jumps" (named after the grenadilla wood used to make clarinets). Brass players learn lip slurs, a new warm-up pattern. The success of your band depends on everyone's effort and encouragement.

119. GRENADILLA GORILLA JUMP No. 1

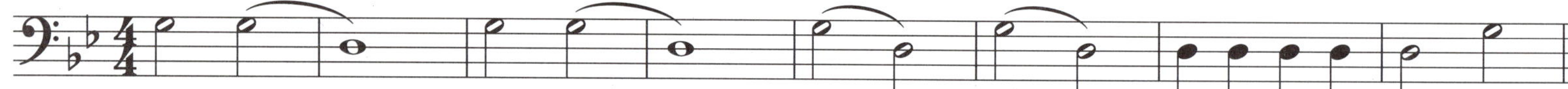

120. JUMPIN' UP AND DOWN

121. GRENADILLA GORILLA JUMP No. 2

122. JUMPIN' FOR JOY

123. GRENADILLA GORILLA JUMP No. 3

124. JUMPIN' JACKS

THEORY

Interval

The distance between two pitches is an **interval**. Starting with "1" on the lower note, count each line and space between the notes. The number of the higher note is the distance of the interval.

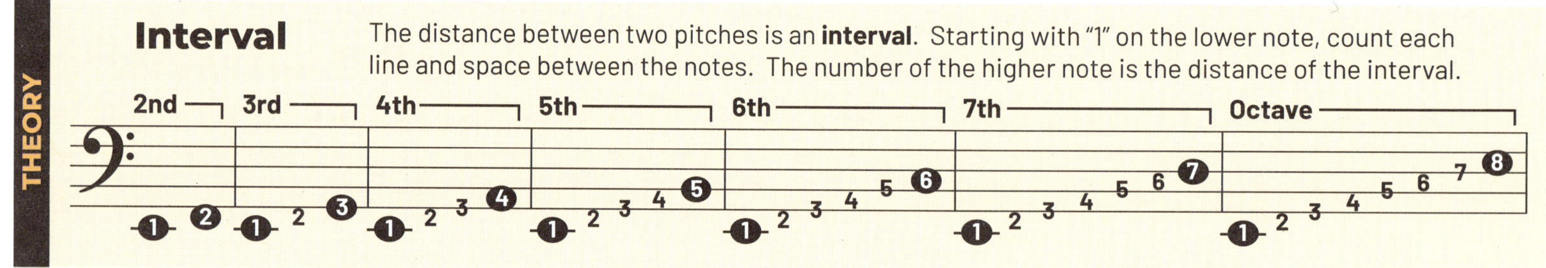

125. ESSENTIAL ELEMENTS QUIZ

Write in the numbers of the intervals, counting up from the lower notes.

Additional bonus songs are available online. See the inside front cover for details.

126. GRENADILLA GORILLA JUMP No. 4

127. THREE IS THE COUNT

128. GRENADILLA GORILLA JUMP No. 5

129. TECHNIQUE TRAX

130. CROSSING OVER – New Note

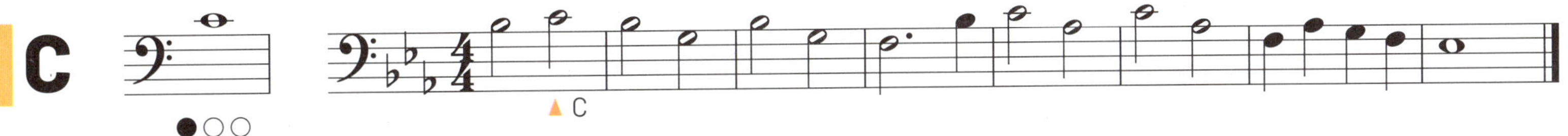

Trio A **trio** is a composition with three parts played together. Practice this trio with two other players and listen for 3-part harmony.

131. KUM BAH YAH – Trio *Always check the key signature.*

African Folk Song

Repeat Signs
Repeat the section of music enclosed by the repeat signs.
(If 1st and 2nd endings are used, they are played as usual – but go back only to the first repeat sign, not to the beginning.)
132. MICHAEL ROW THE BOAT ASHORE
African-American Spiritual
Andante
mf
1.
2.
133. AUSTRIAN WALTZ
Austrian Folk Song
Moderato
f
134. BOTANY BAY
Australian Folk Song
Allegro
mf
f
mf
THEORY
C Time Signature
= Common Time
(Same as 4/4)
Conducting
Practice conducting this four-beat pattern.
1
2
3
4
135. TECHNIQUE TRAX
Practice at all dynamic levels.
136. FINLANDIA
Jean Sibelius
Andante
p
mf
p
1.
2.
© Breitkopf & Haertel, Wiesbaden - Leipzig
137. ESSENTIAL CREATIVITY
Create your own variations by penciling in a dot and a flag to change the rhythm of any measure from
to

138. EASY GORILLA JUMPS

139. TECHNIQUE TRAX *Always check the key signature.*

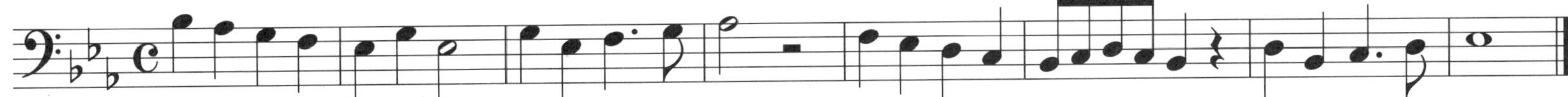

140. MORE TECHNIQUE TRAX

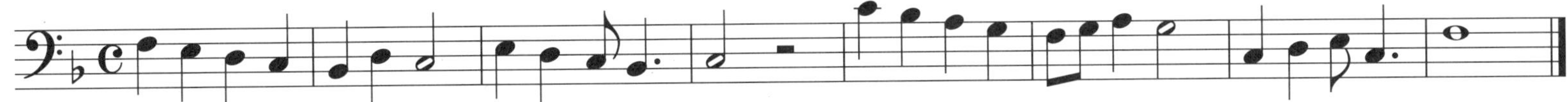

141. GERMAN FOLK SONG

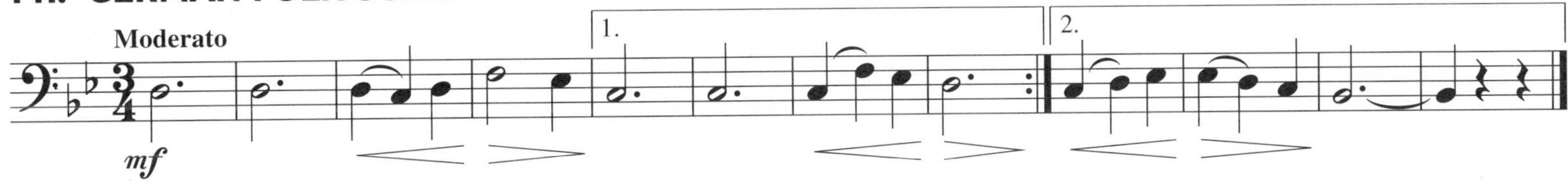

142. THE SAINTS GO MARCHIN' AGAIN

James Black and Katherine Purvis

143. LOWLAND GORILLA WALK

144. SMOOTH SAILING

145. MORE GORILLA JUMPS

146. FULL COVERAGE

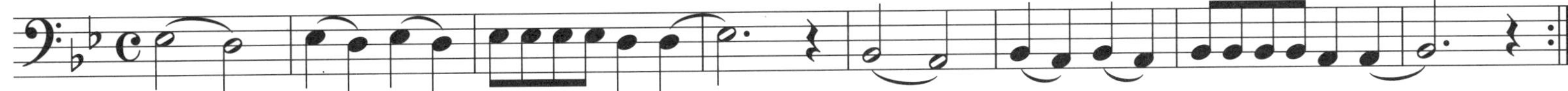

THEORY

Scale

A **scale** is a sequence of notes in ascending or descending order. Like a musical "ladder," each step is the next consecutive note in the key. This scale is in your Key of B♭ (two flats), so the top and bottom notes are both B♭'s. The interval between the B♭'s is an octave.

147. CONCERT B♭ SCALE

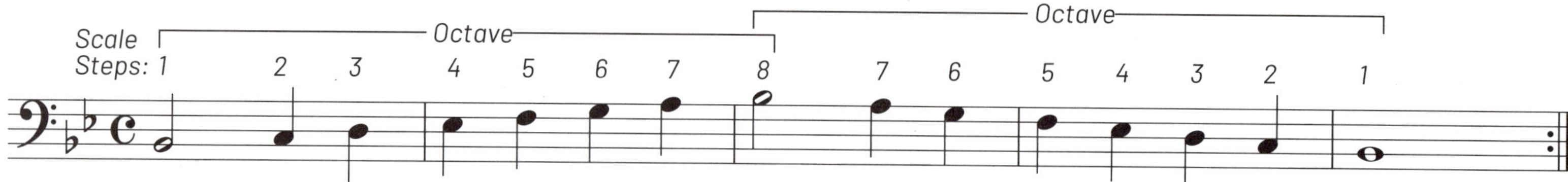

THEORY

Chord & Arpeggio

When two or more notes are played together, they form a **chord** or **harmony**. This B♭ chord is built from the 1st, 3rd and 5th steps of the B♭ scale. The 8th step is the same as the 1st, but it is an octave higher. An **arpeggio** is a "broken" chord whose notes are played individually.

148. IN HARMONY *Divide the notes of the chords between band members and play together. Does the arpeggio sound like a chord?*

149. SCALE AND ARPEGGIO

HISTORY

Austrian composer **Franz Josef Haydn** (1732–1809) wrote 104 symphonies. Many of these works had nicknames and included brilliant, unique effects for their time. His *Symphony No. 94* was named "The Surprise Symphony" because the soft second movement included a sudden loud dynamic, intended to wake up an often sleepy audience. Pay special attention to dynamics when you play this famous theme.

150. THEME FROM "SURPRISE SYMPHONY"

151. ESSENTIAL ELEMENTS QUIZ – THE STREETS OF LAREDO

American Folk Song

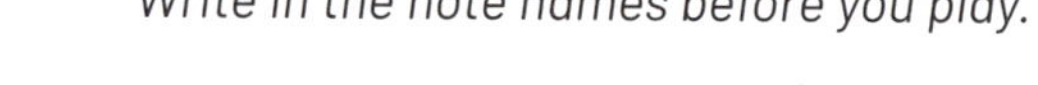

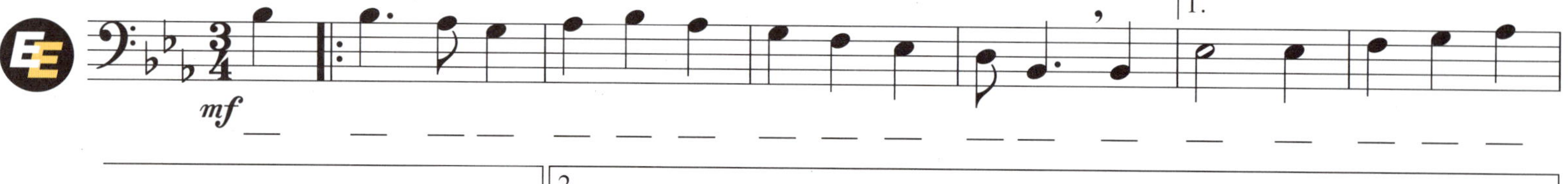

PERFORMANCE SPOTLIGHT

152. SCHOOL SPIRIT – Band Arrangement

W.T. Purdy
Arr. by John Higgins

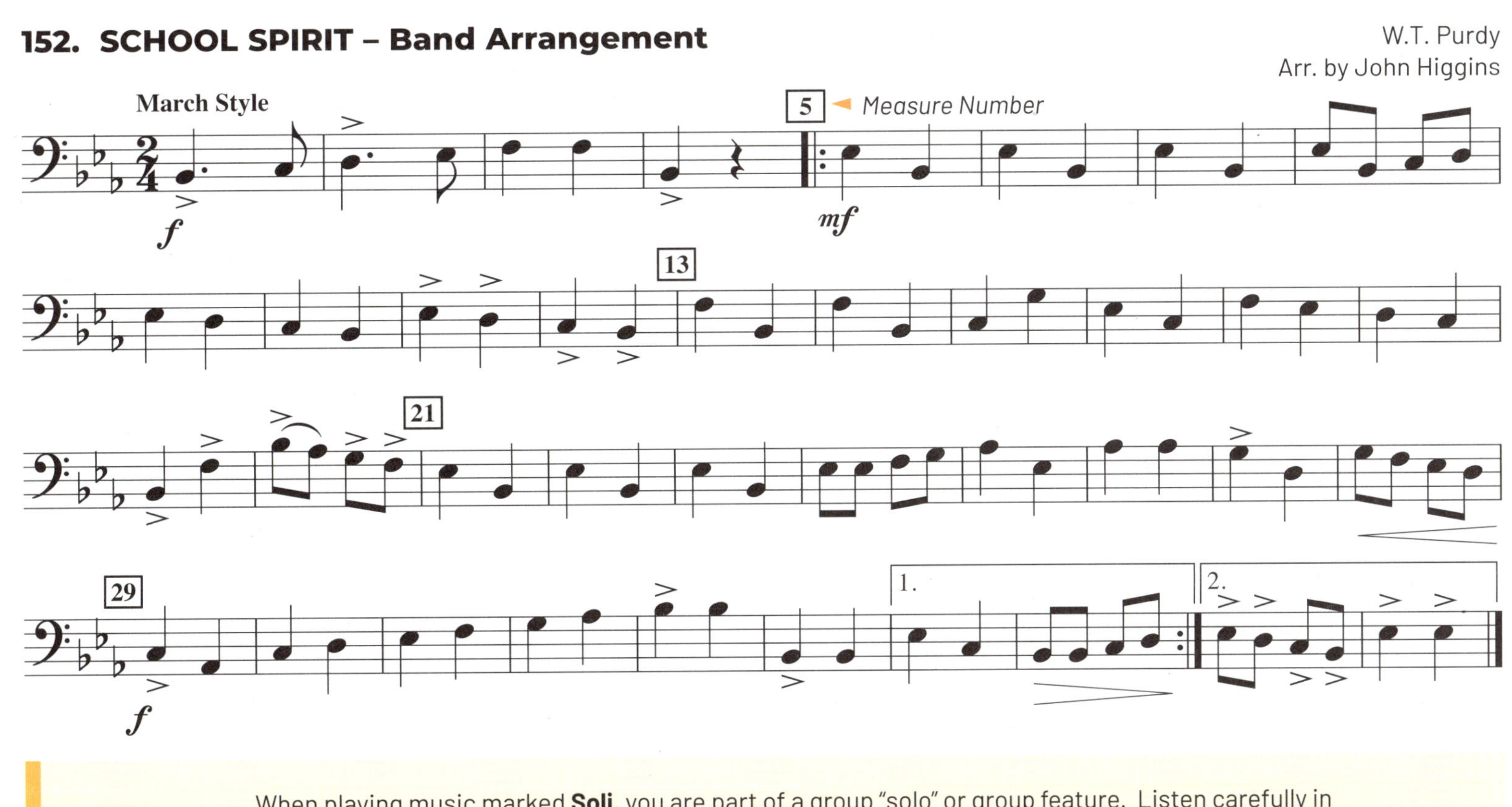

Soli

When playing music marked **Soli**, you are part of a group "solo" or group feature. Listen carefully in "Carnival of Venice," and name the instruments that play the Soli part at each indicated measure number.

153. CARNIVAL OF VENICE – Band Arrangement

Julius Benedict
Arr. by John Higgins

Allegro

DAILY WARM-UPS

WORK-OUTS FOR TONE & TECHNIQUE

154. RANGE AND FLEXIBILITY BUILDER

155. TECHNIQUE TRAX

156. CHORALE

Johann Sebastian Bach

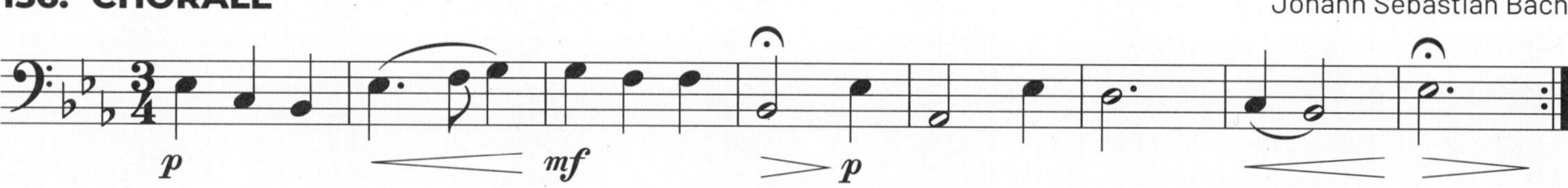

The traditional Hebrew melody "Hatikvah" has been Israel's national anthem since the nation's inception. At the Declaration of State in 1948, it was sung by the gathered assembly during the opening ceremony and played by members of the Palestine Symphony Orchestra at its conclusion.

157. HATIKVAH

Israeli National Anthem

Eighth Note & Eighth Rest

♪ = 1/2 beat of sound

𝄾 = 1/2 beat of silence

1 & 2 &   1 & 2 &

158. RHYTHM RAP

159. EIGHTH NOTE MARCH

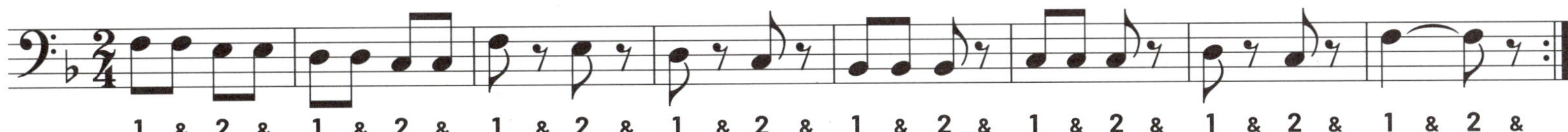

160. MINUET

Johann Sebastian Bach

161. RHYTHM RAP

162. EIGHTH NOTES OFF THE BEAT

163. EIGHTH NOTE SCRAMBLE

164. ESSENTIAL ELEMENTS QUIZ

165. DANCING MELODY – New Note

HISTORY

American composer and conductor **John Philip Sousa** (1854–1932) wrote 136 marches. Known as "The March King," Sousa wrote *The Stars And Stripes Forever*, *Semper Fidelis*, *The Washington Post* and many other patriotic works. Sousa's band performed all over the country, and his fame helped boost the popularity of bands in America. Here is a melody from his famous *El Capitan* operetta and march.

166. EL CAPITAN

John Philip Sousa

HISTORY

"O Canada," formerly known as the "National Song," was first performed during 1880 in French Canada. Robert Stanley Weir translated the English language version in 1908, but it was not adopted as the national anthem of Canada until 1980, one hundred years after its premiere.

167. O CANADA

Calixa Lavallee,
l'Hon. Judge Routhier and Justice R.S. Weir

168. ESSENTIAL ELEMENTS QUIZ – METER MANIA

Count and clap before playing. Can you conduct this?

Enharmonics

Two notes that are written differently, but sound the same (and played with the same fingering) are called **enharmonics**. Your fingering chart on pages 46–47 shows the fingerings for the enharmonic notes on your instrument.

On a piano keyboard, each black key is both a flat and a sharp:

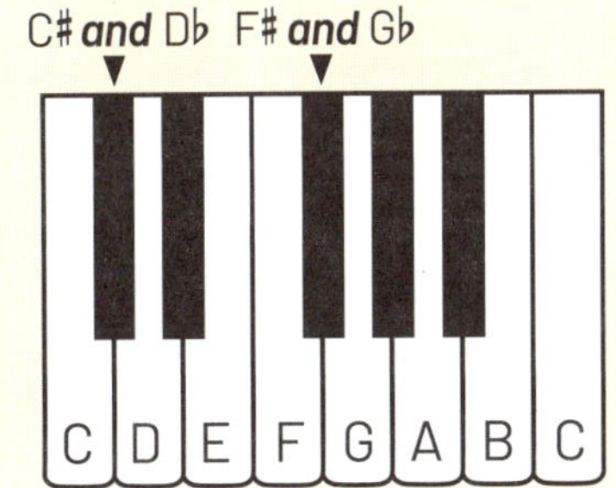

THEORY

169. SNAKE CHARMER

Enharmonic notes use the same fingering.

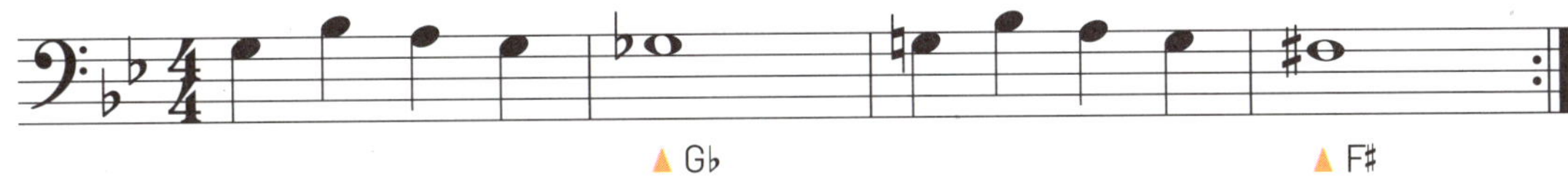

170. DARK SHADOWS

171. CLOSE ENCOUNTERS

Enharmonic notes use the same fingering.

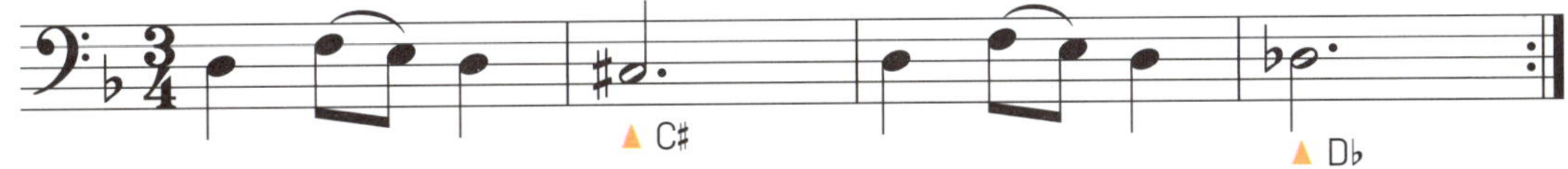

172. MARCH SLAV

Peter Ilyich Tchaikovsky

173. NOTES IN DISGUISE

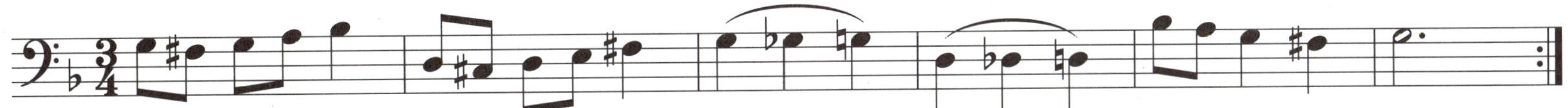

Chromatic Notes

Chromatic notes are altered with sharps, flats and natural signs which are not in the key signature. The smallest distance between two notes is a half-step, and a scale made up of consecutive half-steps is called a **chromatic scale**.

THEORY

174. HALF-STEPPIN'

HISTORY

French composer **Camille Saint-Saëns** (1835–1921) wrote music for virtually every medium: operas, suites, symphonies and chamber works. The "Egyptian Dance" is one of the main themes from his famous opera *Samson et Delilah*. The opera was written in the same year that Thomas Edison invented the phonograph—1877.

175. EGYPTIAN DANCE *Watch for enharmonics.*

Camille Saint-Saëns

176. SILVER MOON BOAT

Chinese Folk Song

Largo

mf

Fine

D.C. al Fine

f

p

HISTORY

German composer **Ludwig van Beethoven** (1770–1827) is considered to be one of the world's greatest composers, despite becoming completely deaf in 1802. Although he could not hear his music the way we can, he could "hear" it in his mind. As a testament to his greatness, his *Symphony No. 9* (p. 13) was performed as the finale to the ceremony celebrating the reunification of Germany in 1990. This is the theme from his *Symphony No. 7*, second movement.

177. THEME FROM SYMPHONY NO. 7 – Duet

Ludwig van Beethoven

Allegro (moderately fast)

A

B

p

p

9

mf

mf

1.

2.

Russian composer **Peter Ilyich Tchaikovsky** (1840–1893) wrote six symphonies and hundreds of other works including *The Nutcracker* ballet. He was a master at writing brilliant settings of folk music, and his original melodies are among the most popular of all time. His *1812 Overture* and *Capriccio Italien* were both written in 1880, the year after Thomas Edison developed the practical electric light bulb.

HISTORY

Additional bonus songs are available online. See the inside front cover for details.

PERFORMANCE SPOTLIGHT

182. AMERICA THE BEAUTIFUL – Band Arrangement

Samuel A. Ward
Arr. by John Higgins

183. LA CUCARACHA – Band Arrangement

Latin American Folk Song
Arr. by John Higgins

PERFORMANCE SPOTLIGHT

184. THEME FROM 1812 OVERTURE – Band Arrangement

Peter Ilyich Tchaikovsky
Arr. by John Higgins

PERFORMANCE SPOTLIGHT

Solo with Piano Accompaniment

Performing for an audience is an exciting part of being involved in music. This solo is based on *Symphony No. 1* by German composer **Johannes Brahms** (1833-1897). He completed his first symphony in 1876, the same year that the telephone was invented by Alexander Graham Bell. You and a piano accompanist can perform this for the band or at other school and community events.

185. THEME FROM SYMPHONY NO. 1 – Solo *(Concert E♭ version)*

Johannes Brahms
Arr. by John Higgins

DUETS

Here is an opportunity to get together with a friend and enjoy playing music. The other player does not have to play the same instrument as you. Try to exactly match each other's rhythm, pitch and tone quality. Eventually, it may begin to sound like the two parts are being played by one person! Later, try switching parts.

186. SWING LOW, SWEET CHARIOT – Duet

African-American Spiritual

187. LA BAMBA – Duet

Mexican Folk Song

RUBANK® SCALE AND ARPEGGIO STUDIES

KEY OF B♭ *In this key signature, play all B♭'s and E♭'s.*

1.

2.

3.

4.

KEY OF E♭ *In this key signature, play all B♭'s, E♭'s and A♭'s.*

1.

2.

3.

4.

RUBANK® SCALE AND ARPEGGIO STUDIES

RHYTHM STUDIES

RHYTHM STUDIES

CREATING MUSIC

THEORY

Composition

Composition is the art of writing original music. A composer often begins by creating a melody made up of individual **phrases**, like short musical "sentences." Some melodies have phrases that seem to answer or respond to "question" phrases, as in Beethoven's *Ode To Joy*. Play this melody and listen to how phrases 2 and 4 give slightly different answers to the same question (phrases 1 and 3).

1. ODE TO JOY

Ludwig van Beethoven

1. Question *2. Answer* *3. Question* *4. Answer*

2. Q. AND A. *Write your own "answer" phrases in this melody.*

1. Question *2. Answer*

3. Question *4. Answer*

3. PHRASE BUILDERS *Write 4 different phrases using the rhythms below each staff.*

A

B

C

D

4. YOU NAME IT: ______________________________

Pick phrase A, B, C, or D from above, and write it as the "Question" for phrases 1 and 3 below. Then write 2 different "Answers" for phrases 2 and 4.

1. Question *2. Answer*

3. Question *4. Answer*

THEORY

Improvisation

Improvisation is the art of freely creating your own melody *as you play*. Use these notes to play your own melody (Line A), to go with the accompaniment (Line B).

5. INSTANT MELODY

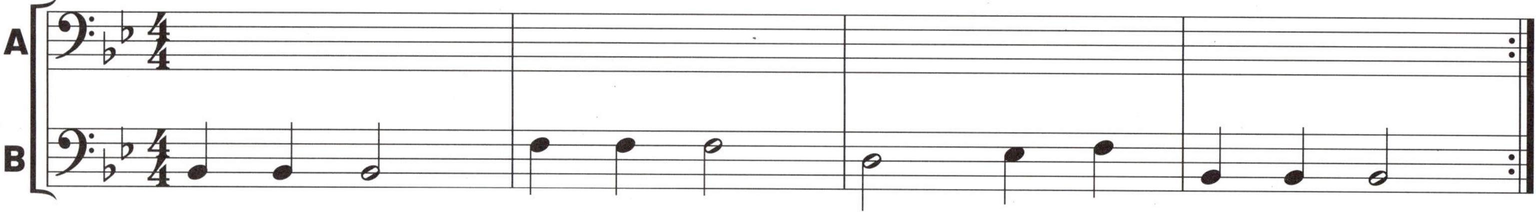

You can mark your progress through the book on this page.
Fill in the stars as instructed by your band director.

1. Page 2–3, The Basics
2. Page 5, EE Quiz, No. 13
3. Page 6, EE Quiz, No. 19
4. Page 7, EE Quiz, No. 26
5. Page 8, EE Quiz, No. 32
6. Page 10, EE Quiz, No. 45
7. Page 12–13, Performance Spotlight
8. Page 14, EE Quiz, No. 65
9. Page 15, Essential Creativity, No. 72
10. Page 17, EE Quiz, No. 84
11. Page 17, Essential Creativity, No. 85
12. Page 19, EE Quiz, No. 98
13. Page 20, Essential Creativity, No. 104
14. Page 21, No. 109
15. Page 22, EE Quiz, No. 117
16. Page 23, Performance Spotlight
17. Page 24, EE Quiz, No. 125
18. Page 26, Essential Creativity, No. 137
19. Page 28, No. 149
20. Page 28, EE Quiz, No. 151
21. Page 29, Performance Spotlight
22. Page 31, EE Quiz, No. 164
23. Page 32, EE Quiz, No. 168
24. Page 33, No. 174
25. Page 35, EE Quiz, No. 181
26. Page 36, Performance Spotlight
27. Page 37, Performance Spotlight
28. Page 38, Performance Spotlight

MUSIC — AN ESSENTIAL ELEMENT OF LIFE

FINGERING CHART

BARITONE B.C.

Instrument Care Reminders

Before putting your instrument back in its case after playing, do the following:

- Use the water key to empty water from the instrument. Blow air through it.
- Remove the mouthpiece. Once a week, wash the mouthpiece with warm tap water. Dry thoroughly.
- Wipe off the instrument with a clean soft cloth. Return the instrument to its case.

Baritone valves occasionally need oiling. To oil your baritone valves:

- Unscrew the valve at the top of the casing.
- Lift the valve half-way out of the casing.
- Apply a few drops of special brass valve oil to the exposed valve.
- Carefully return the valve to its casing. When properly inserted, the top of the valve should easily screw back into place.

Be sure to grease the slides regularly. Your director will recommend special slide grease and valve oil, and will help you apply them when necessary.

CAUTION: If a slide, a valve or your mouthpiece becomes stuck, ask for help from your band director or music dealer. Special tools should be used to prevent damage to your instrument.

○ = Open

● = Pressed down

Instruments and photos courtesy of Yamaha.

E

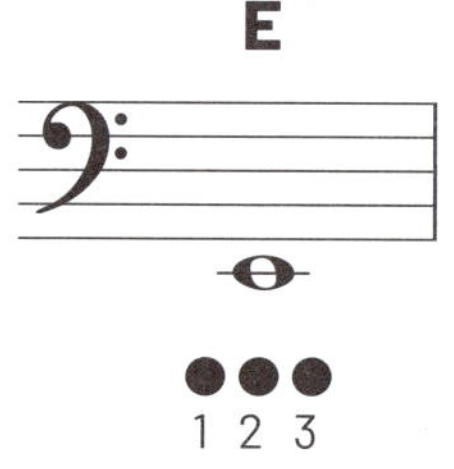

F

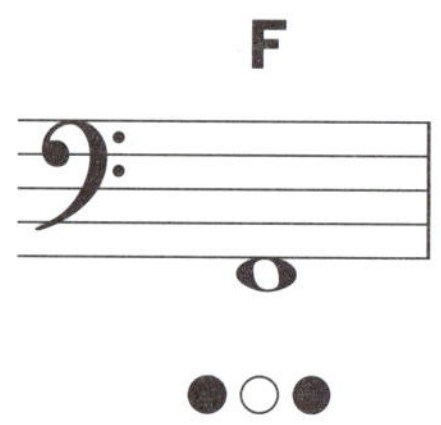

F♯ G♭

G

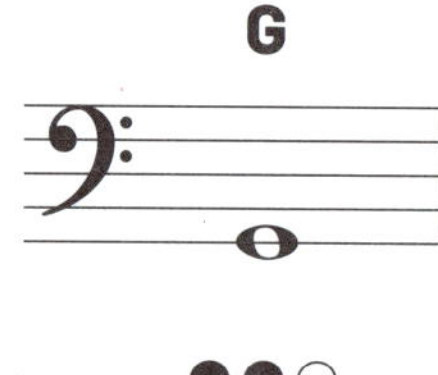

G♯ A♭

A

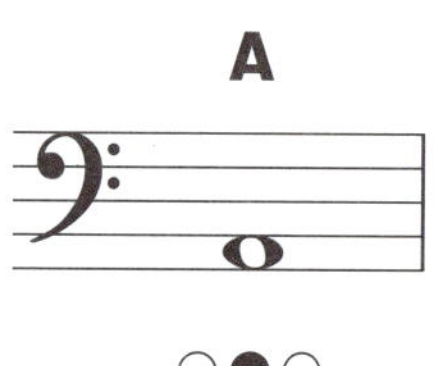

A♯ B♭

B

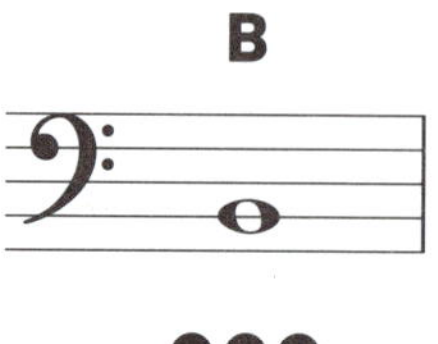

FINGERING CHART

BARITONE B.C.

C

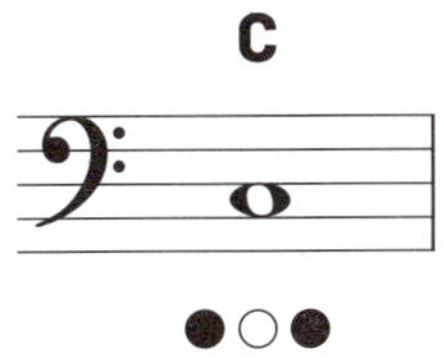

C♯ D♭

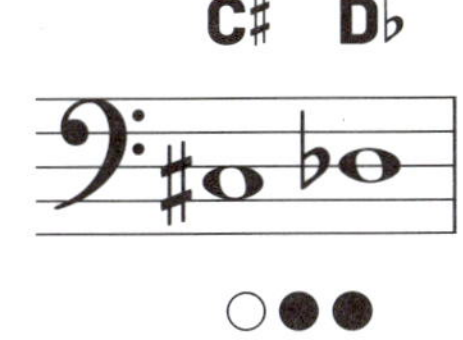

D

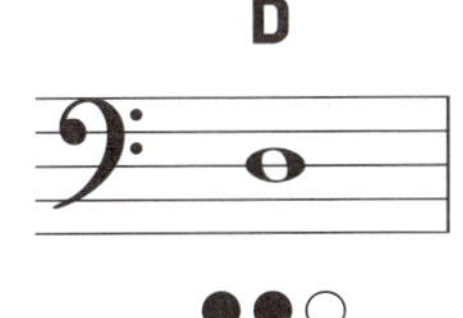

D♯ E♭

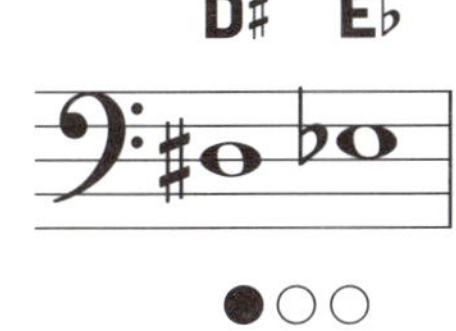

E

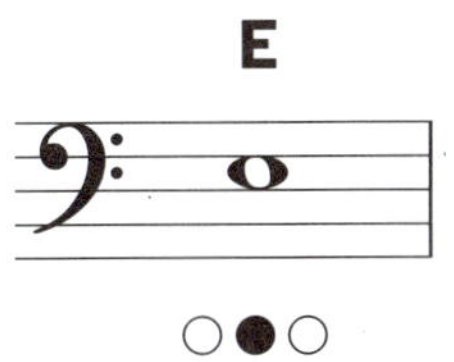

F

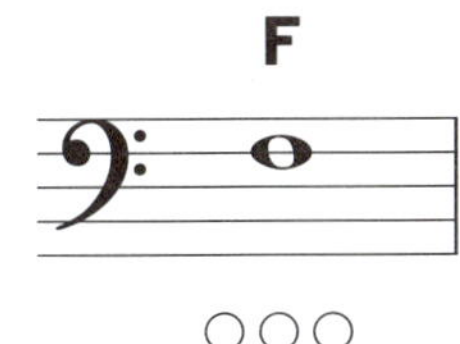

F♯ G♭

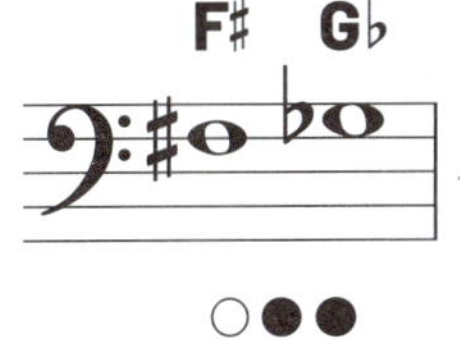

G

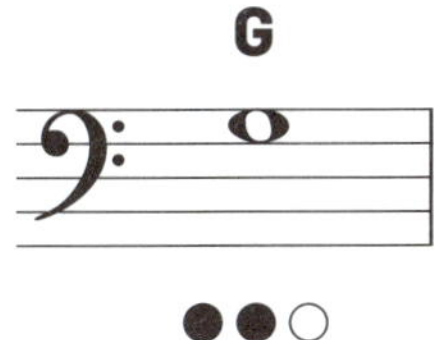

G♯ A♭

A

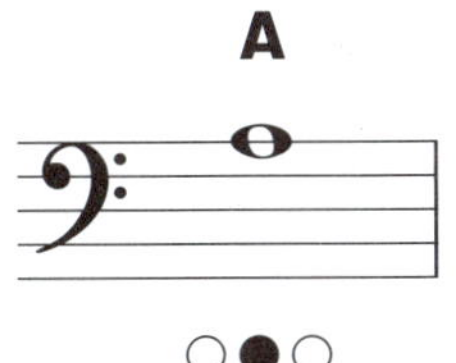

A♯ B♭

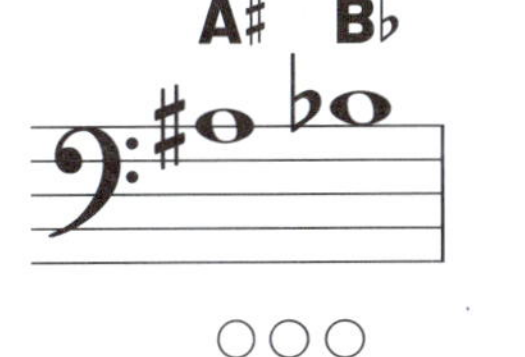

B

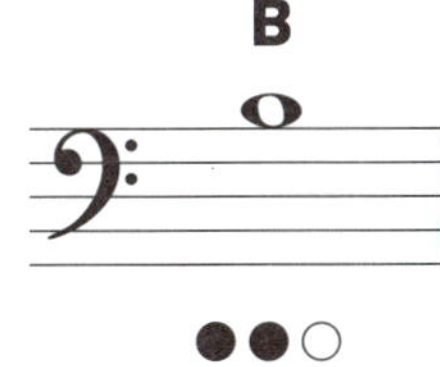

C

C♯ D♭

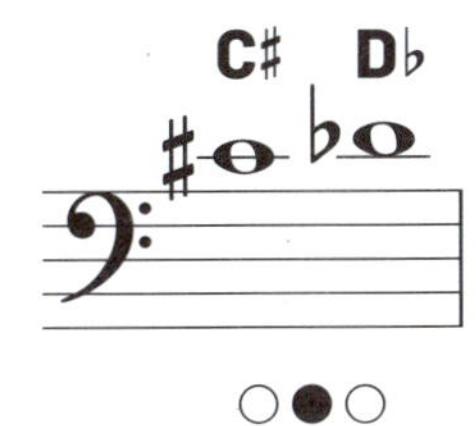

D

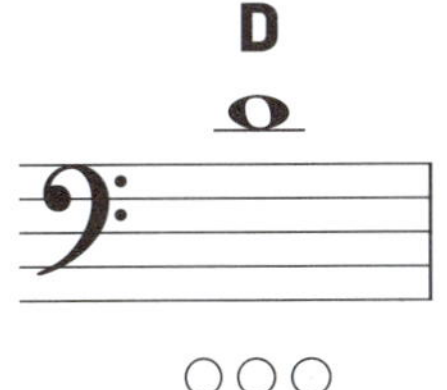

D♯ E♭

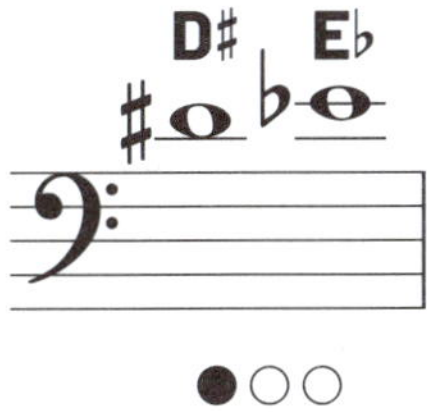

E

F

F♯ G♭

Reference Index

Definitions (pg.)

Composers

World Music